GOOD IDEAS FOR RAISING SERIOUS MONEY

Large-Scale Event Plans

by Sarah Passingham

A Directory of Social Change publication

GOOD IDEAS FOR RAISING SERIOUS MONEY
Large-Scale Event Plans
By Sarah Passingham

Published by the Directory of Social Change,
24 Stephenson Way, London NW1 2DP
Copyright 1995 © The Directory of Social Change
No part of this book may be stored in a retrieval
system or reproduced in any form whatsoever
without prior permission in writing from the
publishers. The Directory of Social Change is
a registered charity no. 800517.

ISBN 1 873860 72 2

British Library Cataloguing in Publication Data
A catalogue record for this book is available from the
British Library

Designed and typeset by Linda Parker
Printed and bound by Page Bros., Norwich

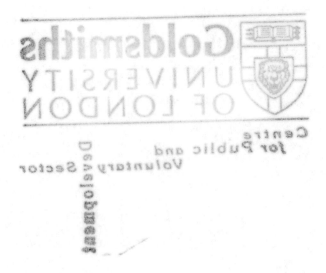

Contents

For Lizzie and Maria,
without whose help I could
have researched and written
this book a great deal sooner.

Acknowledgements

I am grateful to all the people who have helped me put this book together. Several specialists have been accredited within the text, but I should like to extend special thanks to the brains behind the Bergh Apton Experience who wish to remain anonymous – Richard Abel from the Glastonbury Festival, Dick Towler from the Norwich Orienteering Club and many voices on the end of the telephone at the British Orienteering Federation, the Norfolk Churches Trust Ltd, Phil Norton from the Special Charities Unit at Eversheds, Norwich and Helen Chambers from Norwich City Council and Sgt Colin Page from the Norwich Traffic Management Dept – Norfolk Constabulary

Many thanks, also, to Kathy Brown for her help throughout the last three Summers and, as always, the biggest thanks of all go to Dennis whose expertise in editing and child-minding has made this series possible.

About the author

Sarah Passingham has over the past eleven years created, directed or advised on hundreds of events. In her work with Norwich City Council she has been responsible for sustaining the success of large scale traditional favourites such as the Lord Mayor's Street Procession, whilst also helping fledgling events by small voluntary groups to provide entertainment for local people and at the same time to turn a profit for charity or for club funds.

After leaving Art School with a BA (Hons) in Graphic Design Sarah worked as a designer in London. Later, she moved to the field of professional entertainment and worked with many well known rock music acts. She has also been involved with a municipal theatre, first on the marketing side and later as Theatre Administrator.

Returning to her native Norfolk Sarah transferred her entertainment management skills to open air arenas. She now devotes herself to writing, lecture and consultation work and to looking after her two small daughters. She and her family live in rural Norfolk.

Introduction

'*G*ood Ideas for Raising Serious Money*' is the third book in a series of practical guides commissioned by the Directory of Social Change to help volunteers and first-time fundraisers.

Both this book and the second in the series, *'Tried and Tested Ideas for Raising Money Locally'* are intended to be read in conjunction with *'Organising Local Events'*, the first of the series, if you are new to the world of organising charity events.

Organising large scale events is not for the faint-hearted. You cannot hide your mistakes or rectify them in private, as there is no way that you can organise a major fundraising event on your own. You need a cohesive team of people working with you, all of whom need to be efficient, reliable and committed. You, too, need to be all these things as well as determined and assertive with bags of energy into the bargain. If you cannot apply these words to yourself, then give the job to someone else!

Unlike a small event you really can't afford to fail. Of course fundraising events do fail, but the organisers rarely get a second chance and the companies that sponsored them or, worse still, didn't get paid for their services get their fingers burnt too, and are less likely to associate themselves with another charitable event in the future.

Sadly, some charities have acquired a reputation for un-professionalism or for biting off more than they can chew. Several companies and consultancies, that have been only too pleased to help unconditionally in the past, state that the biggest problem that they experience with first-time promoters is that they will not listen to advice.

It is especially tough, when we have been working on an idea for some time, to be told that it must be done differently or that it won't work at all. It is tempting to think that we know our audiences better than the experts from another area. But we probably don't. The skill of being a successful promoter is knowing when to pull out and when to stick to your guns. Being convinced oneself is not enough.

This book will guide you in how to organise whole events

in detail if that is what you want to do, but in many cases, especially if it is your first large scale event, it may be safer to call in the experts in certain areas. Throughout the book you will find suggestions where this might be advisable and why.

Some events are covered by an enormous number of regulations and restrictions and you need to read the relevant publications, where indicated, thoroughly to ensure that you will be running a safe and legal event. Other events need a lot of input from other people, perhaps lending land, houses and exhibits as well as time and energy. All events rely on an audience or participants to provide the funds. You will be working with many, many people – sometimes thousands. Over the years I have been fortunate in making many friends through running all sorts of events and I am sure you will too; so you had better like the human race!

Holding a really large scale event (over 8,000 people, say) is hard in the UK. Unless you are lucky enough to get the use of a covered stadium or other such purpose built building, and there are precious few available, you will be reduced to holding your event in the open air or under temporary structures, or in places such as air craft hangers with all the ambience of the inside of an empty skip. Not only do you have the practicalities of providing energy, infrastructure, safety and other facilities in the middle of a wind swept field to think about, but you have to make your chosen venue operate with smooth efficiency as well as providing the sparkle of the magic and excitement that the audience craves. Don't worry, it can be done!

In this book you will find five ideas that you can use as blueprints to devise, plan, organise and run your own events. I have tried to include events for very different markets to be held in very different locations and for a wide variety of reasons. Many of the suggestions can be adapted for other ideas, and you may be able to mix and match elements to achieve something suitable for your own needs. Remember that these events are from my experience or created from my thoughts. You will need to put your own mark on your own events.

Don't be afraid to ask for advice all along the way. There are plenty of knowledgeable, experienced people out there who will be prepared to help you. Go for the big one! Create an event that will be remembered; have fun - and Good Luck!

Sarah Passingham
March 1995

Your Responsibilities

This section is reproduced here from *'Tried and Tested Ideas for Raising Money'*, they are covered in detail in the first book of this series, *'Organising Local Events'*, which includes information on cutting red tape, how to gain police co-operation and aspects of leisure law. The following points, though by necessity only in outline, should alert you to the danger areas and show you where you need to get further help before you proceed with your plans.

1. You must hold an adequate insurance certificate. Cornhill Insurance provide the easiest and clearest policies available to date – consult your broker.

2. You should be familiar with the basic requirements of the Health and Safety at Work regulations. This is a 'catch all' law that is applicable to anybody who is working with the public, paid or in a voluntary capacity. There is a very clear and easy-to-read publication called *'Essentials of Health and Safety at Work'* which covers all types of activities and gives guidelines on avoiding hazards and what to do in emergencies. It should be compulsory reading for all event organisers planning anything other than a few stalls in a garden.

3. If you employ fairground rides you need to see individual annual safety certificates. You will also need a Site Safety Certificate, which is issued by an inspector who should be a member of the National Association of Leisure Industries. He will want to inspect the site a couple of hours before you open.

4. If you are supplying food and drink you are responsible for seeing that it is deemed fit and safe, even if the public are not paying for it. The *Food Safety Act, 1990* covers all food prepared for public consumption including that manufactured on non-business premises. This could include raffle prizes, free ice-creams or a complete banquet prepared in the village hall. If you are

concerned or unsure about any aspect of food safety or hygiene, contact your local Environmental Health Department for free advice.

5. There is a plethora of licences, permits and bye-laws that you have to apply for or comply with when running events or other kinds of fundraising ideas. I have listed the requirements where appropriate in individual chapters. Some local authorities need more than others (for instance, you might need an official permit to take a vehicle onto a pedestrian area or you might only require a verbal agreement). If a building is licensed to hold so many people, do not try to cram more in to sell extra tickets. The maximum figure is set by the Fire Officer, who assesses the number of people that could exit quickly from that particular premises in a case of fire within a deemed 'safe' time. If you allow more than the licensed number to use the building, you could put everyone in unnecessary danger and obviate any insurance policies. Make sure that you have covered every eventuality well before your event, and when in doubt, ask.

6. Sunday Trading Laws...humph! By the time you read this the laws governing Sunday trading in this country may well have changed. However, to date you need to know what you can and can't sell on a Sunday, even at a Car Boot Sale. Some councils do not enforce the law, others pursue miscreants with a determination to rival a mongoose chasing a snake. If you are bent on selling goods on a Sunday make sure that you are aware of possible consequences in your area. Your local Environmental Health Officer is the enforcing officer so check first.

7. In all cases of fundraising for charitable organisations or projects, check, *before you start planning your event*, that the benefiting charity are happy for you to be running an event or fundraising project on their behalf. You must never use names or official logos without permission. Ensure that you are not in competition with another event for the same cause.

8. As with all appeals, you must open a separate bank or building society account. You have to be seen to be keeping an accurate accounting system and you should always appoint someone as treasurer to check the finances. Never, never allow yourself to be put in a position of suspicion even if you know you are absolutely innocent.

EVENT 1

Street Procession

EVENT 1
Street Procession

Street Processions, Fiestas, Carnivals, call them what you will, merry-making on the move involves the whole community. This is one event where you 'take the mountain to Mohammed'; in other words you decide where the largest crowd of people will or can congregate and arrange your event to travel through that crowd collecting as much interest (and cash) as you can.

By the very nature of the beast, a Street Procession will almost always be held in the centre of a busy town or city, and necessitates the inclusion of a very wide cross section of the public, some of them not very willingly. Generally the procession will be connected with the local authority in some way, even if this is just to include the Mayor or Sheriff to head the affair. It can happen during the day or the evening, it may consist of nothing other than a moving band of people or floats, or it could include a huge range of peripheral entertainment. It may not include a fundraising element, although for the purposes of this book I will assume that this is the main objective. It could be: a one-off; a welcomed annual event; sometimes it celebrates a special date; occasionally it is a specialist local product; and always it will involve local businesses trying to jump on the PR bandwagon.

In discussing Street Processions I will make a few assumptions.

- First, that it is a new event without an annual blueprint to work from.
- Second, that you are planning the event in your home town or city and will not be looking for a venue from scratch.
- Third, that you are a fundraiser for a specific charity looking for an event and that you will form a committee to help you. Many existing civic events, such as Mayor-led Street Processions, allocate a new charity each year to benefit from their efforts, and if your area sports such an event you might be better off spending your time in preparing a really

professional proposal to ensure that your charity is well and truly noticed.

♦ Fourth, that your event will be the only one of its kind in the community and that you will not be competing for space in the calendar. There is only room for one Street Procession in the year in any community, so you might as well make it a big one.

♦ Finally, that as with all the chapters in this book, you should read *'Organising Local Events'* (details at the back of this book) in conjunction with the advice given here. Particulars of obtaining permissions, legal aspects, finding your infrastructure, safety, security, etc. are given in far greater detail than can be repeated here.

Raising funds

A Street Procession may cost several thousand pounds to stage and as with all events from the smallest coffee morning to the largest Band Aid rock concert, you will have to manage a balancing act between income and expenditure.

In this chapter I will show how you can keep funding for the event and collecting for the charity in two watertight compartments. You may choose to operate differently and your organisation may give you more flexibility than I have been allowed in the past, but it is a good system and you can be open to scrutiny in the security of knowing that you are squeaky clean. There is no right or wrong system, as long as you make enough money for your chosen cause to make the work involved worth such an enormous effort, and that you keep your operation strictly legal.

The bottom line is that your income will come from the following three sources and I will explain all in greater detail later in the text:

1. Entry fees.
2. Donations.
3. Sponsorship.

Getting started

You will need to allow a full twelve months to plan your first Procession. Twelve months, that is, from the time that you start organising the thought-through idea. You will need to be sure of the nature of the Procession, what time of year and time of day you plan to hold it, and what it is all for, before you organise anything. If you are reading this with only the germ of an event in your mind, you should either work the idea out by yourself first or form a brain-storming committee to help you before you embark on your actual planning. You can always adjust or change something if it proves to be impossible or impractical, but you cannot ask people to help or get officials involved if you do not have something tangible to describe.

Ensure that you know what you want to achieve. It needs to be more than fundraising, although this will not be far from your thoughts. Read the first two or three chapters of *'Organising Local Events'* to remind you about objectives. It can be helpful to write a formal sort of statement of intent, to ensure that nobody loses sight of the original intention and moves too far away from your original idea. Although you know that if you could not guarantee to raise several thousand pounds you would not stage the event at all, you can put the emphasis on different areas to suit the needs of individuals and groups that will be taking part: a competition for the people making the floats or providing the music or other entertainment; a PR and advertising opportunity for sponsoring companies; news and feature stories and an opportunity to sell more newspapers for the media; a family day-out for the general public; a feeling of responsibility for the volunteer – you can see the sort of thing.

Right at the start of your planning schedule you will need to look at the date and the route. The choice all hinges on your idea. So what is your idea? Sure you've decided on a Street Procession, but what sort of procession, what will your theme be and do you need one? Is it to be during daylight or when it is dark? Which season is most appropriate and will it all be on foot?

The box, right, will give you some ideas to show you what I mean

If you include floats on trucks or lorries you will attract more entries than if your procession is strictly on foot or horse-drawn, and it will draw a larger commercial entry if that is what you want. The procession will not necessarily be any quicker, as in practice there are always hold-ups and walking groups can generally keep up quite well interspersed

---

What's appropriate and when

- Flower Festival with floats – Early Summer, in daylight.
- Christmas Carnival – obviously in December, early evening.
- Lord Mayor's Procession – at your local Mayor-making, in daylight or early evening.
- Hallowe'en – 31 October, in the dark if you are brave!
- Mardi Gras – Shrove Tuesday, all day and evening.
- Firelight Fiesta – 5 November, in the dark.
- Electric Carnival (Floats lit with electric light bulbs) – Mid Summer, late evening.
- City Celebration – Whenever you like.

to name but a few......

between the vehicles. But if nobody walks you could plan a longer route, as it is hard work for some people to walk for more than an hour or two however slow the pace.

Remember that to gain maximum publicity and interest, appropriateness is the name of the game. Link as many local subjects with your theme or with your charity as you possibly can. If you are a children's charity, perhaps you could include several schools in your route; or if you are raising funds to prevent deprivation in a particular ethnic group, make sure you include the indigenous culture of that group and use local representatives. Try very hard to be objective and take a broad view of your idea so that you can prevent antagonising any major group. For instance if you want to hold a Hallowe'en Parade, you might be given short shrift if you try to arrange a route that includes the Cathedral Close; similarly your local Conservative Club might not be too thrilled if you held the major part of a Keir Hardie celebratory carnival outside their building.

On the whole if you want to hold largely politically based events I would advise that a Street Procession is not the ideal vehicle, there are just too many official hurdles to jump and you may not see eye to eye with the authorities. A protest march is different from a Street Procession and the two should not be confused. However, I'm a bit weedy when it comes to being confrontationist, and you might think differently.

Getting started check list

❏ Allow 12 months to plan.

❏ Think the whole idea through before you involve other agencies.

❏ Write a 'mission statement'.

❏ Provide for the needs of different groups.

❏ Decide what form and 'feel' the procession will have.

Preparing for the first meeting

How I used to dread meetings when I organised events before I took a back seat and just advised! The first meeting is always the worst, and can be chaotic whilst people sort out a pecking order and try a bit of muscle flexing, but the sooner you get on with it the better. So, in with both feet and decide who should be invited to attend and who is to be the boss. Actually for the first meeting you should be the Chairman, and don't take any nonsense from those who say otherwise. Vote formally for a Chairman and a Treasurer at this meeting and forget any suggestions for 'rotating chairs' (a phrase that always makes me smile and means different people taking the Chair turn and turn about), it is unnecessary and confusing. You will also need to allocate special duties to specific people. After the first meeting it can be helpful to take a back seat and let someone else be in the limelight, as you need to keep on very good terms with everyone and cannot risk being seen as the heavy-handed ogre!

Decide how often and when you need to meet. Once a month will probably be about right.

Police

The most important group of people involved in a Street Procession is the traffic division of the local police force. Most police forces have a member designated as a community liaison officer, and although you should address your initial request to the Divisional Commander, this is the officer that is most likely to respond to your initial enquiry.

The police can make or break a procession, so you need to listen to what they have to say and keep on good terms. Technically speaking by law you do not have to gain their permission to hold an event on a public highway; in practice they can halt it as soon as it starts by claiming that you are causing an obstruction, a breach of the peace or any number of things. So, whilst you need not grovel exactly, some seriously polite asking needs to go on before you can firm up on a route, especially if you intend closing roads. More of this later.

In a large town or metropolitan city centre you may need police guidance on security, avoiding petty crime and disturbance, car parking and public transport. They will also have to have their say in the Magistrates Court if you intend to apply for a temporary Justices' Licence to sell alcohol.

Local authority

Almost everything you plan to do event-wise will involve someone from the local authority, and a Street Procession can touch on several areas.

You could send an invitation and outline plan to the **Chief Executive** to allow him or her to decide who should attend your meetings. If you observe the correct protocol, this is a must; but my own feelings are that the letter may stay well down the list of priorities and then get sent out to the wrong people. You could be landed with someone from an admin. department who keeps putting the kybosh on all your ideas because they may have less vision.

Try encouraging the **Head of the Leisure and Community Services Department** (or equivalent) to be on your side. On the whole this section of local government tends to be less bureaucratic and more creative than the purely administrative side, and you may find that the department has a helpful **Promotions Officer** who can guide you through the red-tape. But don't let them take over your event unless you want them to.

One council officer should be enough to represent all the different departments but you should be aware of where the involvement is coming from in case you need to chase different people. You could find that you will be talking to people from **Planning** to allow you to close off roads, the **Licensing Officer** to allow you to hold a collection, the person in charge of **Parks and Public Gardens** if you want to include these in your route, an **Environmental Health Officer** if you plan to have entertainment anywhere where you might need a Public Entertainments Licence, and also to make arrangements to sweep the streets or collect litter and make extra toilet arrangements. Environmental Health are also in charge of registering food stalls and enforcing the Sunday Trading laws. The **Works Department** will be involved if you need areas roped or barrier-ed off or extra lighting, the **Mayor's Office** if you intend to have a civic presence, and possibly other departments that I haven't thought of perhaps if you are near the sea or plan to use an historic building and so on.

Chamber of Commerce, Trade and Industry

Business people are always on the look-out for a new way to get their companies' names to the forefront. Your street procession will have a captive audience and can be very attractive to the world of commerce. Instead of button-holing a few prominent business people, and they are always the same few who have grown cynical with the years, take the broad sweep. For once you can use the scatter-gun approach, but in this case it should be down a carefully aimed barrel. Your local Chamber of Commerce will have a membership ready tailored to your needs and you will only have to make the one invitation to the Chamber Director. Make sure that you send your letter well in advance of your meeting, as he or she will have to raise the idea of sending a representative to your committee at their next monthly meeting, and they will have to choose someone who is prepared to be available over the whole year.

The Chamber of Commerce can help on several levels. They will have many member companies that enter floats in national processions and will produce a very professional standard of work adding to the quality of the event. Other companies have social clubs who will like to enter locally prepared efforts. Many companies will welcome the opportunity to be associated with your cause and might be prepared to sponsor certain elements in full. Most commercial operations can be persuaded to take out advertisements of varying sizes in programmes or around advertorial text (an advertisement disguised as editorial) in the local newspapers. In Norwich the Chamber of Commerce came in with a 50% involvement to help organise the whole Lord Mayor's Street Procession. They took on the financial overview and undertook overall organisation of the float entries and musical entertainment, both of which were run as competitions. You may not want such a blatant association with Mammon, but it could be useful as a once-only involvement to help get a potentially annual event off the ground.

Media

It is helpful to have a journalist or a member of a newspaper or local radio promotions team actually on your committee. Contrary to popular opinion, journalists are human beings and get caught up with the excitement of the whole event just like anyone else. What better way of ensuring that every little PR opportunity, every little extra story gets milked for all its worth than having someone attend a meeting one evening and write an article direct for the media the next.

By including a representative of the media you will ensure that you design the best possible publicity schedule for yourselves and be able to hand a large part of it over to a professional who will be paid by someone else. The only proviso is that your event must be big enough to warrant their costs.

The benefiting charity

I am aware that all sorts of concerned people will be reading this book: those individuals who are unconnected with any particular charity but who have a passion to raise funds for a certain cause; groups in the community who regularly get together to fundraise for different charities such as the Lions Clubs or Round Table; appeal managers working for specific charities who are looking for ideas to suggest to the different regions; or regional fundraisers looking for a large event to bring in a target figure.

If you are fundraising for a registered charitable organisation, you should get permission from the benefiting charity before you do any fundraising on this scale; and unless you, the organiser, are employed by the charity, it would be courteous to invite a representative of that charity to be a member of your committee.

Not only can someone directly involved with the charity guide you across any potentially dangerous political minefields that you happen to stumble upon, but they probably have the back-up of a well-oiled publicity machine that can supply the media with extra editorial and you with all sorts of attractive freebies for the day – such as leaflets and information to raise the level of awareness of their cause. They may also be able to pull strings to gain access to some all important VIPs that you will need later in your planning.

So it is not only courteous, and not just very useful to get the benefiting charity's permission, it's also sensible – since under the 1992 Charities Act, a charity can seek and obtain a legal injunction to prevent unauthorised fundraising by third parties.

So, what have we got for your first meeting? A member of the local police force, an officer from your local council, a representative from the Chamber of Commerce, a journalist and someone from the benefiting charity (unless you are taking on that role), and yourself of course, acting as Chairman. Six people that can comfortably meet in someone's house or in a back room of a pub. You will also need someone with access to a typewriter or word processor to take minutes and act as a secretary for the committee; this could be one of the committee members or a volunteer. Try not to get roped into doing this task yourself, as you will not have time and will have far too many other things to think about.

And, naturally, you also have a pretty well formed idea about the event itself.

Preparing for the first meeting check list

❏ Do not procrastinate

❏ Select a chairman for the year

❏ Plan how often you should meet

❏ Invite members from police, local council, Chamber of Commerce, media and the charity

❏ Employ a voluntary, reliable secretary

First decisions and the way forward

By the end of your first meeting:

◆ You should have agreed on a route and the date and time to hold your Procession.

◆ You will have confirmed your theme or the reason that you are holding the event and whether you plan to have a competition and prizes.

◆ You should also have an idea of which organisations you can ask to steward the event, where you plan to sell alcohol (if at all) and some of the additional entertainment.

◆ If you have time, try to work out a very rough schedule of tasks and further discussions.

◆ Decide, also, when and where your meetings are to take place (read Chapters 4 & 5 in *'Organising Local Events'* for further details).

Remember to have discussed the all important 'mission statement', and make sure everyone involved agrees and understands it.

Route

Your route should aim to go where most of the people are. There are two ways to achieve this. You can collect the people artificially together in one place, say a park, by holding another attraction there or, and this is my favourite, you go to where people have already amassed in some numbers. A busy city centre is ideal.

It will be an unusual town or city whose officials will allow you to hold an event down main streets during normal shopping or working hours, so the most likely times will be Friday or Saturday evenings or any time on a Sunday.

Allow the police to guide you in deciding a route; but if you hanker after a particular street and they are less than enthusiastic, pursue your idea until you hear a sensible reason to avoid it. The police, like all of us, have other motives (the ubiquitous hidden agenda!) and it could be that they haven't looked at the possibility of turning a one-way street into 'another-way' street just for the event, or that they feel that the pavements are too narrow to hold the crowd safely. Maybe you could offer additional stewards or pay for three or four Special Constables to patrol there.

When you have your route firmed up, it is sensible to write to any public services, such as bus companies, who use the roads as part of their business to inform them of your intentions and promise that you will keep them fully informed. You can have plenty of time at this stage to negotiate or make other arrangements if it causes serious upsets.

It is a good idea to find a large area – a car park or playing field is ideal, or a straight, wide residential road failing all else – for all your floats and groups to gather together before the start. You should allow for two or three hours use before the start time at least, especially if you plan to hold the judging of any competitions before they move off.

Similarly, at the end of the route, there must be room for floats to disgorge passengers and pay over collection money to a central collection point, without causing too much of a traffic jam before all the vehicles disperse. Again a park or school playing field would make an excellent finish point, but any wide road or perhaps a roundabout might do as well.

If the civic buildings are attractive, have a balcony or a pretty garden on the road, try to arrange for the route to pass the front. You can design a VIP viewing area or you could arrange for judging to take place from a special tent or raised platform. The more you make the civic dignitaries feel important and really vital to the whole event, the more likely you are to be able to repeat the Procession another year. Invite all the sponsors too and you will make everyone happy. If the Town Hall is a ghastly monstrosity with a sheer concrete front, perhaps your main sponsor has a better office building that you could take advantage of. Consider what the procession passes as well as the most direct route from A to B and exploit the best that your locality has to offer. Follow the river so that people can watch from boats, pass under a bridge which can be strewn with flowers, circle a central garden area where you can hold a fair or drive slap bang through a pedestrianised area (as long as it is wide enough) just to give some novelty value.

Once you have firmed up on your start and dispersal points and the route between, you will need to contact the Planning Department of your local Council so that they can have their say and post advance warning notices at the appropriate times. Permission must also be sought from the appropriate landowners, if your start and finish is on land other than the public highway.

The Engineers Department could be another port of call as they should hold the annual plans for works by all the utility services. This means that you will be informed of any major digging works that might threaten your route or, having got the route confirmed, the combination of planners and engineers should be able to prevent the road being dug up on the day of the event... well, this is how it works in theory. In practice it is often a very different story. I was involved in helping to organise the Norwich end of the Norwich Union RAC Classic Car Rally where five starting points of nearly one hundred cars all converged on Silverstone for a grand get together. A couple of days prior to the date gas engineers dug a hole 6ft deep across the whole width of the road which was intended to be our major route out of Norwich. We got round it, well over it really, by laying huge metal sheets over the hole but it took some organising and I nearly used up an annual supply of charm getting the work for free! So you need to watch for the unexpected.

However, your route will not be cast in concrete, metaphorically speaking, until the Planning Officer has taken a report to Council and had it ratified by the Members. Only at this stage can you begin to publicise your plans.

Date and time of day

Very often your theme or celebration will suggest the date if not the time as well. But there are occasions where you will have a completely free choice. To gain the most from any event you need to choose a time when the most people will be attracted to participate or spectate. School holidays and half terms can be tricky, as families often go away and any activity instigated by the schools cannot be seen through to completion. Avoid Bank Holiday Mondays like the plague for the same reason. Obviously, the Summer will offer more rain-free days and the warmer weather is a great incentive to families to get out and about. However, you must be prepared for rain in the UK, and I've often managed events in a drizzle that seemed not the least affected by the lack of sunshine.

In my experience early Summer events are much more popular than later on in the year. The public seem starved of outside entertainment in May and June, whereas they have become blasé by August and September. Autumn and Christmas evening events have an excitement all of their own, and the combination of nightfall, bright lights and frosty weather can weave magic that you cannot achieve at other times of the year. So don't be too sure that your procession must take place on a warm Summer's day.

Daylight or dusk? Decide on the length of your event (discussed later in this section) and work backwards. Suppose you plan to finish with a brass band playing for 15 minutes and you need to finish in daylight, even in June you won't want to go much beyond 9.30pm at the outside. So 9.30pm onwards is out of the equation. The police have said that as it is a Sunday you can operate any time after 11.00am. But you decide that people need to have their lunch first and come out afterwards, so you can plan your event any time between 2.00pm and 9.30pm. The procession will take two hours and allowing for the band playing and clearing up afterwards, you need to start at 7.00pm at the very latest. The floats can take 2 or 3 hours to all arrive and get organised so that takes you back to 4.00pm, and you can see how the time will more or less arrange itself. Of course, a light bulb carnival has to take place in the dark, so you need to plan a different time of the year, perhaps September or October to ensure that you get several hours of darkness before everyone is ready to push off home.

Some smaller processions or parades can be successfully interwoven with the regular road-users. This is a great advantage and means that you need not go through the rigmarole of getting roads closed off, and you could run your event during a normal working day if you wanted to. However, you will be restricted to using roads that experience only light traffic; your procession will have to travel at the same speed as the other users, which means that everyone must travel in some form of reliable vehicle, be it motorised or horse-drawn, and you will not be able to have a foot patrol collecting money from the passers-by. The police will dictate the time of day that you can use this method as you will have to avoid obvious rush hours or school collection times, and they will expect you to be out of the area within a short time.

Even as I write this, I feel that even if you come up against great difficulties in getting roads closed you should still pursue this objective. Remember, think big and splendid. Don't be intimidated by your lack of experience, you have all the advice you need right here in this book and the others in the series!

Allow yourself enough time to get all your parade through. With nearly one hundred floats in the Lord Mayor's Street Procession in Norwich travelling barely two miles, it still takes from 6.45pm until after 9.00pm for the last floats to pass the dispersal point. The procession moves at the speed of the slowest participant who might be a six year old in a majorette troupe, and at times comes to a complete standstill (time for a horse to eat an entire double hanging basket, flowers, moss, banner and all, during one incident that I witnessed). To give you an idea of the snail's pace that a street procession moves at, I regularly would walk the full length of the entire column four or five times during the course of the evening without walking particularly fast. We are talking about one mile an hour here!

To reiterate, you need to consider your subject matter, the probable weather and temperature, how long it will take from start to finish and how much time you need before and after for judging or other attractions. Does your idea need darkness or daylight? And will you have to clear up completely straight after the event or can you leave it until the next day?

Procession and theme

Nearly all modern street processions are derived from the carnivals held in some Roman Catholic countries to celebrate the season before Lent. In fact the words Mardi Gras come from the French meaning 'Fat Tuesday' this being Shrove Tuesday when you feast before the start of the period of fast that starts on Ash Wednesday. The Mardi Gras takes place principally in New Orleans and includes music, dancing and parades of floats and costumed merrymakers in the streets. It is from these wonderfully extravagant carnivals and fiestas that we get our inspiration for street processions. Unfortunately, or perhaps I should say fortunately because they often result in injuries or even fatalities due to the lack of restrictions, our own activities are severely limited by law as well as our unkind weather, and perhaps not a little by the more reserved British temperament. But they do tend to be safer.

The Notting Hill Carnival is about as close as we get in the UK to the traditional form of processions seen around the world, and we all know the headache that this event gives the London Metropolitan Police.

As stated earlier in this chapter you can use all motorised transport for your floats, and at its simplest a parade can consist of purely visual tableaux carried on the backs of trucks or lorries through the streets.

Generally floats are created by building scenery or models on flat-bed lorries. Sometimes up to twenty people act out a scene all dressed in colourful costumes, on other floats they support massive puppets or models. In Lincoln as in towns in Holland the floats are completely covered in flower heads, each depicting a vast picture or even a working model. In other parts of the country floats are covered in glowing light-bulbs looking for all the world like a huge fair ground travelling through the centre of the town.

You can include horses or even dogs pulling vehicles and coaches, or costumed people riding singly or in groups. Vintage transport is often a great attraction, and many companies maintain pre-war delivery trucks or brewer's drays for just these occasions. Fantasy often plays a part and you could well find the Royal Mail entering Postman Pat in his van or the local cinema entering the Batmobile.

Many events are led by something other than a line of floats. You could hold you procession in May and lead the parade with a May Queen travelling in a horse-drawn carriage – very magical. In Norwich the route is cleared by the VIP van transporting the judges to their dais. Then the Lord Mayor's Dash is started; this is a road race of runners from a local athletics club. The Town Crier then sets off ahead of the Procession followed by a traditional dragon puppet called Snap who 'works' the crowd. Finally the main Procession moves off headed by the Chief Constable's car; a Rolls Royce bearing the Mayor and family; and a Scottish pipe band fronting the first float.

Most events include music and this greatly enhances the atmosphere and excitement. Bands can ride in style on a lorry as a sort of mobile bandstand complete with chairs and music stands. Again in Norwich we use a Caribbean steel band transported in this fashion. Massed bands can march, military style, between floats along the road or you can use recorded music amplified through loudspeakers either on floats or along the route. Somehow the fact that there are so many sources of different music doesn't seem to matter at all as long as there is at least one 'silent' vehicle between each musical one.

Individuals on unicycles, jugglers and fire-eaters are all good for a bit of variety as are dance and majorette troupes. Motorcyclists in formation are another a popular attraction.

You may have a clear idea of what you want to include in your parade, but have you thought about a theme? Some events will suggest it for you, a parade to celebrate your charity's 100th anniversary will naturally have an historical theme and can tie in nicely with local events that may have happened last century. A Christmas procession just has to include carols, the nativity and Father Christmas. But what about the Street Procession that happens sometime during the Summer for no special reason other than it is a very good way to raise funds? You could just have a free for all; but whilst this may work for the first year, you will find that participants really do like to have a subject matter to work within. Absolutely anything will do. Some of the themes I have worked with or seen include Nursery Rhymes, Trade and Industry, Fables and Fairy Stories, Partnership, All Things Green – to name just a few. You could think of some much more interesting ones I am sure, how about 500 years into the Future, Animals and Birds, Local Legends, The European Connection, or something that is particularly pertinent to your cause.

Whatever you decide, make it broad enough for people to come up with all sorts of different ideas, you don't want five or six floats all depicting the same ideas. Also, although your message may be strong and very serious such as civil war and starvation in Africa, try to keep the event light-hearted – however much you feel people need to know what is going on. By all means have an accessible information stand somewhere in the centre of the town for interested members of the public to gather information and where they can ask questions. But keep it low key, it is a sad fact that the public would rather have a good time and be kept separate from the reality of hardship, even though they are giving money to prevent it.

Competitions and prizes

If you run the procession as a competition or a series of competitions, you will add an extra element and zest to the event. People like to contend with each other for the best floats or the cleverest interpretation of the theme. An annual cup and some valuable prize money adds to the contest. From your point of view it is a great way to ensure that the standard of entry is high and provides a good carrot to encourage entrants to follow the theme. If you need a few rules, and you will, automatic disqualification from the competition is a powerful incentive to read the guidelines carefully and stick to them.

It is often more fun to have several prizes as well as an overall 'Best Float'. You could have a competition within each class or you can include more specific prizes such as 'Best Float involving Young People', 'Best Hand-held Puppet' or perhaps, say, if your charity encourages protection of the planet you could include 'Best Float using Natural Mobility' or 'Best Float built using Recycled Materials'.

Judging should take place at the start, before the floats have had time to get bedraggled along the course or spoilt due to wet or windy weather. If you judge somewhere on the route the floats cannot display their prizes and your judges cannot make a decision before the end, you have the added difficulty of getting the prizes to the winners when they are tired and hungry and want to disappear as quickly as possible.

Your judges should be mobile, either on foot or in a van. Perhaps you could arrange for an open sided truck to be decked in bunting and sport a few chairs, to carry the judges up and down the lines of floats and then on to the VIP stand somewhere on the route before the rest of the procession move off.

Have some large sheets of card made up with the name of the prize and a space for a rosette. These can be held or displayed in the window of the cab after the judging and during the parade. Cups and rosettes will be carried high and shown off, and the local press will have an opportunity to take some pictures whilst everyone is still fresh and full of bounce.

If you include marching bands or dance troupes you could run separate competitions for these. These will have to be judged on the move, and you will need a judging dais erected along the first ten or fifteen minutes of the route. You will encounter several difficulties. Firstly, these competitions are not as light-hearted as the rest, after all many bands and troupes consider themselves to be semi-professional. You will need to find an official judge capable of judging each element properly and according to the

The way forward check list

❑ Allow the police to guide you in deciding a route.

❑ Remember to start and finish on a wide area.

❑ Contact the Planning Office.

❑ Firm up on a date and time.

❑ Do you need to close roads?

❑ Allow about 1mph for the procession to travel.

❑ Make your theme broad enough to give everyone a chance.

❑ Decide on who or what will lead the procession.

❑ Decide on the musical content.

❑ Plan any competitions.

rules. Secondly, the problem of presenting prizes exists when you judge on the move. Lastly, you need to ensure that all musicians and troupes entered for the competitions are in the first half of the parade, so that a decision can be made before the end. You can then announce the 1st, 2nd and 3rd prize winners at the VIP stand if it is near the finish, and even present the prizes as and when the winners come through, having radioed the results down in good time beforehand. It is safer to send the prize money with the pay cheques after the event.

Organising the entertainment

There is a lot more to a street procession than just the parade. You are aiming to attract as many people onto the street as possible, and having got them there you must keep them there for as long as it takes to give them a good time, so that they want to repeat the experience another year and so that you can relieve them of as much cash as they are prepared to part with. That might seem mercenary and tough, but what else are you putting yourself through this agony for if not to raise as much dosh as you can!

You are creating a fantasy world out of familiar surroundings – just for a few hours – where everything is fun and laughter and people can leave their problems behind and view their work or shopping place through very different eyes. The atmosphere needs to be safe but exciting, hard work but very enjoyable, and give the illusion of being all for free. Only at the end will people realise that they have paid for their day out, but you need to give them such good entertainment that they decide that it was good value for money; and like the awkward toddler, we will all do more if we think we are in control.

To hold people on the streets and keep their hands in their purses, you need to keep the entertainment coming fast. Never let up for a second, provide refreshments round every corner and remember the whole family. Try not to leave any gaps in the proceedings where people start to get restless and the mood dips, they might realise that they are getting cold and their feet hurt, toddlers in pushchairs start to whine to go home and middle aged businessmen wonder what on earth they were thinking of coming out to something so frivolous.

The floats, the music and the extra curricular entertainment, as it were, all have to be planned carefully, balancing artistic presentation with practicalities. In some towns it simply will not be possible to have street entertainment 'en route'; you may have to end in a large field or park and hold a fair as a focal point. Other cities may have grand central squares that lend themselves to street theatre and a static band.

Ask the pubs to apply for extended licensing hours, if necessary, so they can remain open during the whole of the proceedings. This way you can arrange for the public to have refreshments and for toilet facilities to be available, and you have not had to part with any money to provide them. Of course your charity will not benefit directly from all that extra beer being sold, so cash in yourselves and arrange for a beer tent or two to be erected in a public garden or at the edge of a car park (see the Chapter on Licences, Bye-laws and Booze in *Organising Local Events*' for further details).

If you have the space, get a local scaffolding company to build a public grandstand for elderly people or those with walking difficulties so that they can view in comfort. Allocate a small area for under-5s with a gentle roundabout, a couple of swing boats and a baby change room. How about some merchandising stalls? I once organised one procession wearing a T-shirt bearing the logo of the event and the date on the front and sporting the slogan *The Buck Stops Here*' in huge letters on the back. Every float leader wanted one for themselves; so there's one idea for free!

Buskers, jugglers and other people with circus skills are all good for milling about in the crowd and being ready to step into the road if a nasty gap appears in the procession.

If you have a large park nearby organise side shows or book some fairground rides, and if your event goes on into the evening end with a bang by arranging some professional fireworks or a 'son et lumiere' show. There is nothing quite like a dramatic pyrotechnic display for rounding off a day's entertainment satisfactorily.

Floats

If you invite everybody and anybody to enter a float, you will get a good response but a very varied standard of entry. For a large event you must consider sorting the entries into classes even if you do not plan to hold a competition. In this way you can restrict certain areas and build up others to give you a balanced procession. It gives you control, an excuse to deny entry and some useful 'packages' with which to encourage sponsorship.

The most obvious division is between 'commercial' and 'non-commercial'. With this simple classification you have allowed yourself the possibility of charging a pretty hefty entry fee (say £100+) for the commercial entries and a much reduced rate for non-commercial participants who could well be put off by anything more than about £15–£20. If all your rates were at the lower end of the scale to attract everybody, you might be denying the event its true market value.

Many commercial entries will be nothing more than a gigantic advertising display, a couple of spanking new cars with bunting in the company colours depicting their logo, or even simply a mobile stand of the kind that you might see at a trade fair.

My feeling is that these floats are not entering into the true spirit of the event and can spoil the carefree atmosphere of the day. However, and it is an important 'however', they are often the companies with the most money to spend and think nothing of paying £100 to enter, another £400 for a special full page advertisement in the programme, and if you are really lucky, contributing a silver cup or even the prize money. So it is important not to alienate them altogether. If you now divide the commercial floats into sub-categories of 'themed' and 'un-themed' with only the themed being allowed to enter the competition (if you hold one), you can now ensure that you will encourage people to make something creative and unique to your event, whilst allowing room for those who still insist on doing it their way.

Now to the non-commercial entries. This section will often comprise of other charities using the opportunity to make people aware of their work. If you wish to maximise your fundraising, you have to make it very plan at the outset that these groups are collecting for your cause and not their own. You can't stop people handing out badges and leaflets though, and you probably have to shrug your shoulders and accept it as part of the deal.

Other groups that will enter this section are community centres, schools, scout and guide groups, youth clubs, all sorts of leisure clubs for after school, over 60s, mums and toddlers, sports and arts; you name it, they'll be there! Some of these groups will be well established and have a large membership to draw on. They will often have access to equipment and funds to rival any of the commercial floats. Others will be a casual collection of people who can barely afford to enter a Mini let alone a lorry, and often feel that they would like to enter but think that it is all too large and professional for them.

A few years ago, in Norwich, we opened a Community Group class for groups of three or more who wanted to enter on foot. It was a great success, and you will be surprised how much time and effort residents on a big housing estate or members of a social club might put in over the weeks preceding the event to produce some wild and exotic and beautifully built hand held puppets or costumes that are every bit as visually dramatic as the large floats. You will know your own community so make sure that you include opportunities for everyone to take part.

Music

Some processions start and finish with marching bands or musical floats. Others have music playing alongside the route. Your town or city may dictate the best way to include your music. If you have lots of wide open spaces and a short route, it might be more attractive to seat your musicians and confine them to one spot. For a more protracted route with narrower streets and lots of corners, it might be safer and more enjoyable to have your musical elements as part of the procession. Intersperse the bands, on foot or on wheels, between the other entries. It is a nice idea to head the parade with a really good professional band that are used to marching and can keep the pace moving briskly.

If you plan to pay bands to enter, and this is the usual form, you may have to keep all the expensive groups within the first fifty floats so that they can be sure of finishing within an hour or so. If they are positioned towards the back, they know that they will have to keep playing and marching until the bitter end which could be a couple of hours or more. You might lose the good will and not be able to book them again and, worse still, you could find yourselves being charged double for the extra time playing. Always check with the band leader when you book them if the fee is charged by the hour or for the whole event.

Street entertainers

You can go through the entertainment directories or local agencies and book professional entertainers. Personally, I think it is more ethical to involve the indigenous population. When I ran events I always kept my eyes open for a good street act. If I saw a talented busker when I was shopping locally I would ask if he or she was interested in being part of the coming street procession. If the answer was yes, I made a note of the name and a contact address. You can build up quite a file in this way. It has several advantages. One, they are all personally known to you and you are aware of what you are getting. Two, they cost far less than a career entertainer and you have no agency fee to pay either. Three, they often have a local cult status and pull their own crowd in a way that is impossible with imported people. The disadvantage is that they may not turn up on the day, but then, neither may your bought in act if they have to travel far.

Try to book wandering acts with no more than three in the group. They are far more versatile and can entertain the whole length of the procession by wandering gently up and down. They can go where they are needed rather than relying on people coming to them.

Use a mixture of acts, fire-eaters, jugglers, singers, clowns, magicians and puppeteers. Almost everyone has a place. If anything, perhaps you should err on the visual rather than the vocal which might end up getting a little lost in with the general hubbub of activity.

Static entertainment and refreshments

Entertainment in this section falls into two groups. Those who charge a fee and those who pay you. Entertainment that provides a general enjoyment such as a barrel organ or piece of street theatre is generally booked by you and paid for. Things such as roundabouts where children pay for a ride or somebody puts money in a slot to make something work, need to pay you for a pitch. You don't get the money that they take from the crowd, but you do take a flat fee in advance to allow them to carry on their business at your event.

Visit local fairs and fetes to see what is available locally. You may need to do this the year before you plan your event, many side shows and rides get booked up to a year in advance for popular weekends. Try to visualise where each stand will go before you book it. Space will be at a premium unless you are very fortunate, and you should not fall into the embarrassing

---

Organising entertainments check list

❏ Keep the entertainment coming, avoid gaps.

❏ Arrange for pubs to extend opening hours.

❏ Arrange your own beer tent.

❏ Remember problems of disabled people and special groups.

❏ Consider merchandising.

❏ Plan spectacular finale.

❏ Try to balance the entries and give everyone a chance.

❏ Consider how you include music.

❏ Keep professional musicians in the front half and check fees.

❏ Use local street entertainers.

❏ Sell pitches early to ensure stalls are available.

❏ Consider putting all the extra entertainment out to tender.

hole of having too many side shows and nowhere to put them.

Your local Environmental Health Department should be able to give you a list of registered mobile food stalls, or you can take pot luck and advertise in the local press for people to apply for pitches. Again you should collect the pitch fees well in advance of the event to ensure you get paid. Look at the section on Trade Stands in *'Organising Local Events'* for more details.

If you would like to get shot of organising anything other than the procession itself you can cheat! Invite tenders from local groups that already collect for charities (Lions Clubs, Rotaract, Round Table, etc.) to use your event to run extra entertainment for themselves. This is what I mean. You set aside an area or space for their exclusive use – they could run a fairground for instance – all the money they make goes to their chosen charity but they pledge to give you, say, £500 of the take. You make your choice according to the attractiveness of the idea and the amount they pledge to your cause.

. . . .

Behind the Scenes

Organising a large event like a street procession involves a tremendous amount of hidden activity, both before and on the day itself. You will need to think through the financial aspects very carefully. The publicity should operate according to a planned schedule and not just when the mood takes someone. Infrastructure and services all have to be considered and booked. Volunteers need to be mustered and trained. And a complete list of duties including legal requirements needs to be drawn up, allocated and put into some sort of time-scale.

Permissions and Applications

Before you go very far down the line of planning your event there are certain hoops that you must jump through before you can proceed.

◆ We have already talked about the need for a report to go to the Council to formally apply for **road closures**.

◆ You will need to apply for a **Street Collection Permit** from the Administration Department of the same council. You may need to book the date up to year in advance and should certainly allow three months for the application to be processed.

◆ **Signs** to direct floats to the collection space and signs warning the public that the Procession is imminent will have to be arranged. The RAC, the AA or certain private Events Service

33

companies can work out the best places to situate these, have them made, apply for planning permission, and site them for you. Again, you will need to apply several months in advance.

◆ **Permissions** may need to be obtained for you to use private property such as car parks, school playing fields or company property.

◆ Don't forget to speak informally to the **Mayor's Office** if you want him or her to play a part. Make sure that the civic dignitaries are not booked for another function that day.

◆ You should book a hall or large room to hold a **public meeting to explain the rules** and give out entry forms at least eight weeks before the event.

◆ Make sure that you have arranged adequate **insurance** and that it is operating during the set up time as well as the day itself.

◆ Apply for any **Liquor Licences** that you might need for beer tents. You need to allow two or three months in case you have a problem and have to re-apply. Find out when the licensing sessions are held and make sure you don't miss one by a day or two, or you may have to wait another three weeks for your application to be heard.

◆ If you intend to hold a special attraction with music and dancing either outdoors or in an unlicensed building you may have to obtain a **Public Entertainments Licence**. Procedures for cutting all this red-tape and applying for licences are laid out in *'Organising Local Events'*.

Infrastructure

You might think that very little infrastructure is needed for a parade. After all, the venue exists, the road is already there, as are the pavements and the collection and dispersal points. People do not have to be kept out as there are no tickets, and by the same token there is no need for turnstiles or ticket booths. All of which is absolutely true.

But – and you knew there would be a 'but' didn't you? – where several thousand people are involved (up to 40,000 is the latest 1994 police estimate for the Norwich procession) in a limited space there is always the potential for safety problems, and an audience often has to be contained within a safe area. Sometimes that means restricting access by the use of crash barriers or ropes. Provision has to be made for the emergency services to operate in exceptional circumstances.

So, let's take it from the top. At your collection point ensure that there is plenty of room for lorries to arrive and park up without obscuring vision in the road. Contain the public to one side or the other of all the lines of floats. If necessary create 'pavements' by roping off a central area for use by floats only. Ensure that you provide a separate space for parking coaches (many of the bands will arrive by bus or coach) and horse boxes. Horse drawn vehicles should not arrive earlier than thirty minutes before the start time as the animals can become restless waiting around in a constricted space.

If there are no public loos available, make sure that you import a couple of temporary toilet blocks.

In the summertime it is helpful to have a refreshment stall available. You can expect floats to begin to arrive two if not three hours early. Some people actually make most of their floats during that time, and drinks and biscuits are very welcome as well as an added source of income.

Use a van or truck as your point of contact. I always used a Renault Trafic which gives you good headroom and you can leap into the cab and drive it all around the route as and when you need to; but there is bound to be something better still by the time you are reading this, just make sure you don't have to keep your head bent all the time you are working from the back, you will end up with a very stiff neck. You should also be in constant communication with your team by radio, but more of that later.

At some point during the evening before your event you should mark out where each float or band or troupe has to stand. Yellow road marking paint can be obtained from the Highways Department. It comes in an aerosol can and is very effective for writing numbers on tar-macadam or grass. Later in this chapter I will show you what information you need from each entry, one vital piece of knowledge being the amount of space each group takes up. Measure each length carefully and allow a good twenty feet either end to compensate for mistakes and turning in for parking.

If your event is taking place at night you may have to make arrangements to have additional lighting or for the regular street lights to be lit longer than usual; this goes for the whole route. Many councils save money by switching these off after eleven o'clock in certain areas.

Further down the route you may find that roads become rather narrow, and you need to use crowd control barriers to prevent the spectators from getting in the way of the floats and, more importantly, floats from squashing spectators. If the route includes the odd planted roundabout, it is politic to rope the whole area off as they are popular vantage points, and there will be very little evidence of pretty flowers after hundreds of feet have squashed the life out of the last blade of grass.

All your barriers and ropes will have to be dropped in piles around the route during the hours before the roads are closed. If you are borrowing barriers from the local council or police force, you may be able to ask them to make the drops. If you are hiring barriers from an independent source they will be dumped in a pile, the supports separated from the gates. Arrangements will have to be made to bolt them together before you start, and a flat bed truck with a driver and six or eight volunteers made available to load and deliver. Don't forget that they will all have to be retrieved and unbolted at the end of the event. The barriers, that is, not the volunteers! Mind you, after a few pints...!

Next you should arrange for a viewing platform to be built for band judges to sit on, unless a convenient balcony presents itself.

The VIP dais can be cleverly devised from the same vans that you used to transport the judges around the floats. When they travel down the route ahead of the procession they can arrive at a prearranged point, and with the judicial addition of some more chairs, can become a VIP vantage point. If you plan to invite more VIPs than can be accommodated on a couple of vans, then you will have to arrange some other form of platform.

At the dispersal point your objectives are to relieve the collectors of all the cash that they have collected from the crowd, and to allow the floats to drive off as quickly as possible. A basic register should be kept recording the number of the float and the name of the leader or driver, who should be in charge of handing over all the coins.

Assuming that you have chosen a fairly wide space to finish your procession, and you would be well advised to do so, arrange your crowd control barriers to make two large funnels or you could use a natural junction. The bands and dance troupes, who will not have collected money, walk away through one funnel leaving the floats to go through the other. If you have a very large area two funnels for floats allow the operation to carried through all the faster. Don't allow people to leave the floats at this stage as you should keep the area exclusive to the procession stewards. Extra bodies running about could well end up under the wheels of lorries or horses which would be catastrophic.

Speed is of the essence here, otherwise you will cause a bottleneck that will have ramifications for the whole line of the procession behind you. Forget all about trying to count money at this stage. Using at least six helpers, grab each collection bucket as it comes through and shy the contents either straight into the back of a windowless truck, or if you are not close enough use metal dustbins – the handles come off plastic ones as you try to lift them! You will need a strong person with a shovel to shift the coins around inside as the truck gets full! And you may need to line it with plastic sheeting to prevent coins falling through the gaps in the floor. Remember to choose a vehicle that is capable of taking heavy loads. After all you will be collecting anything up to £10,000 in small change.

At the end you may be planning a finale of some sort. If this is to include fireworks or something else where the public is to be kept separate you may need to use crowd control barriers here too. As the procession moves away from the start point you can send the truck to collect barriers that are no longer serving any function and redistribute them to where they will be needed at the end. You may save a considerable amount of money by this double use if you are hiring barriers.

Finally, make sure that the float drivers are directed out from the town centre and away, possibly to a park or recreation ground on the outside of the town to dismantle the float and drop off passengers.

Stewards

The efficiency and safety of your event hangs on the quality of your stewards. The ultimate steward is a Police Constable and your local police force will insist on having some on site. Each police force has its own policy about charging for a police presence. In Norfolk it costs £62.00 for the first two hours and £31.00 for each hour or part of an hour thereafter. Special Police Constables are free (1994 figures). You may be lucky and be charged nothing, but you cannot guarantee it. Each year the financial squeeze presses harder as our police forces are condemned to more cuts, and you may find that where once you enjoyed their support for free next time you could be looking at a pretty hefty bill. Don't assume; always check.

The police aside, you need one steward for every five floats. In practice, bearing in mind that you will have bands and troupes interspersed throughout the procession, each steward actually looks after ten groups.

The first steward should walk on the right side of the road, the second on the left, the third again on the right and so on for the full length of the procession. Ideally four stewards should be in radio contact with you and the reception van where booking in takes place and all the numbers, official collecting badges and stickers are given out.

Before the procession starts the stewards' job is to guide each float or group into their starting position as marked on the ground. They should also informally 'police' the crowd to prevent people acting in a dangerous manner, answer questions and report anything that gets out of hand to a Police Officer.

The stewards who accompany the first floats can become cash gatherers when they reach the funnels at the end and remain in situ or get replaced in shifts by other stewards as they become tired or need a break.

Depending on the type and quantity of any extra entertainment that you are providing you may need extra stewards dotted around the route as permanent posts. You will certainly need stewards to guide pitch holders to their sites and check that they are who they say they are.

If you provide a disabled people's viewing area you will have to steward this, at least at the beginning to ensure that it isn't populated by all and sundry. You could make this a 'pass only' stand.

So where do all these stewards come from? Unless your charity has access to many, many fit young men and women, you may have to look to local groups to help you. In the main I would avoid using under 18s or individual volunteers as they are difficult to co-ordinate. Groups that I have used in the past include the Venture Scouts and a particularly successful bunch, who were members of an amateur radio club providing their own radios which was a great asset. You will also need radios for the driver of the lead car, yourself, a member of the police if they cannot hear your wave band, and perhaps a base office where people can leave things or messages and which acts as a central meeting point.

If your volunteers do not come with radio attached you can hire radios by the day from companies that you will find listed in the *Yellow Pages*.

Behind the scenes check list

❑ Make applications and plan well in advance:

    12 months book VIPs and celebrities

    12–6 months Street Collection Licence

    9 months road closures

    3 months signage

    3 months Liquor Licence

    3 months Public Entertainment Licence

    2 months public meeting hall

❑ Crowd control barriers.

❑ Bumbling pins and ropes.

❑ Delivery truck, if necessary.

❑ Judging dais or open sided vans.

❑ VIP platform and chairs.

❑ Strong-axled truck.

❑ Mobile toilet blocks.

❑ Squirty road paint.

❑ Refreshment stall.

❑ Direction signs.

❑ Check lighting needs.

❑ 1 steward to every 5 floats.

❑ Extra stewards according to your periphery entertainment.

❑ Stewards for grandstands.

❑ Radios, 4 for procession stewards at least, plus 2 or 3 more.

Marketing

A good part of your marketing will take place in the local press and perhaps on local radio and if you choose a journalist who knows her stuff to be a member of the committee it should be self perpetuating to a certain extent.

Pricing can be a major potential headache, but because there are no tickets you will save yourself this one.

One thing is for sure, you cannot assume that anybody knows anything. Whole swathes of the population do not listen to the radio and in my experience, when I speak to the hundreds who claim they have never seen my posters, they must go around with their eyes shut too!

Remember, marketing is information. But people cannot cope with too much in one go. You need to trickle feed the press, the public and participants and to this end you will need to work out a schedule to remind you, if nothing else, when to action things and not to forget anything vital.

Decide your plan of action fairly early on and book adverts or write press releases at the appropriate times. If something new happens or you manage to book a famous person at the last minute, it all helps to keep the interest fresh.

Public Relations

The most important thing to remember is why you need to collect £x,000. It is not enough to say that it is for Save the Children, Oxfam or to save small animals from a fate worse than death. You need to have a project, preferably a local project, that needs a specific amount of money so that people can see the final result of their efforts.

If you have something pretty diabolical that you need to improve, change or put right, so much the better. If you saw Ann Mackey's 'That's Life' Russia Appeal for the children's hospital near Leningrad in the summer of 1994, you will recall the overriding memory of the revolting, unsanitary bathrooms and operating theatres. Television pictures showed patchy bacteria-ridden walls with the tiles hanging off, orange rust and black mould mixed with decaying effluent in the children's bathrooms, so that you could almost smell the stink through the screen and dark, grim wards housing sad, pale children. Anybody who saw the 'before' pictures could not get to the appeal 'phones quick enough.

It is before the event itself that you can hit the public with the real reasons for your appeal or educate them about your cause.

On the day they really want to have a good time and forget about the horrors. But horrors help to sell the idea first.

Advertise a telephone number for people to ring for application forms on every press release or make it known that forms can be collected from your local Tourist Information Office, Charity Shop or wherever. Most of Chambers of Commerce have a monthly magazine, arrange to include an application form as an insert in the edition that goes out three months before the event.

Three or four weeks before the event plan to hold a public meeting and invite anybody who has had their float entry accepted. A public meeting is a very up-front way of disseminating information. People have a chance to ask questions and you can press home a few rules that need emphasising. Start the meeting with a brief but succinct outline of the project for which you are fundraising. It can help to have a celebrity or civic VIP to give a few rousing words to get the gathering into a positive frame of mind. Aim to have the whole thing over in about 45 minutes, and push the point that each float has to supply as many collectors working on foot as they can.

As the date of the procession draws near, you might need to consider personally informing the residents near the start point of any plans and apologising for any inconvenience caused. In Norwich this area is closed to traffic two or three hours before the procession starts, and naturally people who live in the road have to know details so that they can arrange to park their cars outside the restricted area or at least be resigned to going on foot if they want to go out. A personal letter should be delivered to each individual house outlining the precise times of closure and when you expect everything to be back to normal again.

Finally a letter to the local radio station might be useful indicating alternative ways through the area so that they can broadcast it throughout the day. This also serves as an extra reminder to people that the event is on.

Publicity

Newspaper advertising can be very expensive. I have rarely paid for advertising for any event as I usually manage to work out some mutually beneficial deal, and there is no reason why you should not suggest the same thing. If the local press prints your programme of events the day before and on the day itself as a free supplement to the newspaper, you will get a free programme and they will sell more papers.

That is not all... If you are prepared to release your list of float entries, and remember at least fifty percent will be commercial, they have a valuable list of people to try and sell advertising space to. In return you can negotiate free or discounted advertisements on the run up to the event.

Don't go mad over printing posters. You do need some but let the press carry most of your advertising. Give a poster, some leaflets and a car sticker to everyone who attends the public meeting. They can put them up in their local shops or community centres and you can concentrate on the central areas. Don't forget the libraries and public buildings.

> **Marketing check list**
> ❏ Publish a realistic project and your target figure.
> ❏ Keep hard facts about your project to the beginning of your campaign.
> ❏ Advertise a contact for applicants at every opportunity.
> ❏ Hold a public meeting for entrants.
> ❏ Write a personal letter to residents or shops most inconvenienced.
> ❏ Send a press release to radio stations giving alternative routes.
> ❏ Negotiate with the press.
> ❏ Have some posters, but don't print more than a couple of hundred.

Finances

I have always been lucky when running events to have a powerful, well oiled financial machine looking over my shoulder pointing out the weak points. You may be lucky too and have the structure of a large charity behind you, but you still should know how the money goes round. To those of you who understand the world of banking and finance, I apologise for my 'paint by numbers' approach. I do not intend to be patronising but I am certain there are many people who suffer from number dyslexia, just as I do, and need to be helped through the rudiments.

The first thing to point out is that it is helpful if your banking is done within the rather larger parameters of an appeals committee account rather than opening a unique account for this one event. This means that you can keep your *organising money* totally separate from your *project money* which has the advantage of being able to roll over funds to another event, add to it or even sit on it for a year until you decide to run another procession. There is more about this in Book 2 of this series, *Tried and Tested Ways of Raising Money Locally*.

This is easy to understand if you think of the event in two parts. First, you have the costs of running the show and the income from the float entries. This is one part. One should balance the other out. It won't, but I will show you how to achieve that a little later in this section. Second, you have the street collection that is taken on the day. You can realistically expect to have an average of 25p given from each spectator. 40,000 people could donate £10,000 in just a few hours. Quite incredible, but true! This is your project money and kept quite separate from the running costs of the event. Keep in mind that the general public have dipped into their pockets specifically to contribute to the published appeal. My feeling is that you should not then use those donations to pay for the procession costs.

Make sure that floats provide their own buckets and receptacles. Legally they are supposed to provide sealed tins, but we never have and the police seem to accept the exceptional circumstances. It would seriously slow things up if people had to drop each coin into a slot, quite apart from the problems of changing all the tins as they became full. Participants must fix an official sticker to the outside of the bucket and wear an official badge though, to prove they are collecting for the charity.

Sponsorship

In the last section I explained that I would describe how to make the income and expenditure balance. The answer is sponsorship. 'Ugh', I hear you groan. 'Nobody sponsors things any more'. Not true. Not as much as they used to, maybe. But its still out there if you present the right package. Look at your largest single expense. It could be a firework display as the finale. You won't get much change out of £2,500 for an 8 to 10 minute firing. That is a frightening amount of money to go up in smoke, but the promise of a spectacular ending really helps to keep people on the streets and spending.

Divide your expenditure up into bite sized chunks and make a list with the finale as your flagship. Offer the list to local companies and organisations and let them pick their own area to sponsor. Of course all sponsors have their names published in the programme, and you can offer any amount of advertising along the route if you don't mind advertising banners slung over barriers. Ask sponsors what they would like in return for their money and decide if you can comply. However, don't sell yourselves short. A street procession is a very prestigious event and an association with a charity has good PR value these days.

Areas that are good for sponsorship include hiring or borrowing of vehicles. Ask the supplier direct, if possible; you might just get a splendid Bentley complete with chauffeur if you are lucky. Then there's security, which means barriers, ropes, radios, etc. Perhaps an alarm or fencing company might help you there. Other infrastructure – maybe you could find a building company willing to donate the toilets for a day from a site that is not working at a weekend or during the evening (I'm not sure that somebody would want to sponsor this directly!) Road signs. Public address systems if you use them. Prize money. Cups and rosettes. The costs of each individual band. Other street entertainment. Publicity costs. Posters and adverts. Stationery. Insurance. The cost of a secretary. Postage costs. Hospitality costs. All these items can be packaged and offered to an appropriate sponsor, and the least attractive ones will have to be paid from your income.

Of course, if you get more sponsorship money in than you have to pay out (come and work for me!) then you have the flexibility to choose whether to make an extra payment into the project fund or keep it as a float towards the costs of organising another event as described at the beginning of this section.

Finances checklist

❑ Keep donations separate from running costs and float income.

❑ Use appeal fund account rather than specific event account.

❑ Use official stickers and badges.

❑ Offer sponsorship 'packages.'

❑ Ask for help 'in kind'.

Emergencies and safety

If you gather thousands of people together for whatever reason, you are bound to have a few medical emergencies and some criminal activity. If you include vehicles, horses, alcohol and excitement especially after dark you increase the risk enormously. Your job, along with guidance from the police and other services, is to minimise that risk as far as possible, and to enable any problems that do occur to be dealt with as quickly as possible with as little disruption to the rest of the event as is necessary.

You should book the Red Cross or St John Ambulance to attend the event. St John will bring their own emergency vehicle and you should make a central parking spot available to site it. You may have to have a meeting with a representative from the official Ambulance Service to work out which is the best route for them to attend the most crowded areas of the procession. The Fire Service may wish to meet with you also to work out alternative routes if they need to get their tenders to a fire during the event. You may be blocking their way to the quickest route. Barriers should not be erected in such a way that emergency vehicles cannot get through. Allow 'gate ways' at strategic points along the route and wide areas to allow vehicles to turn round.

Keep the crowds well away from fireworks and if pyrotechnics are planned read the chapter on fireworks in *'Organising Local Events'*.

As far as petty thieving, pickpockets and vandals are concerned, instruct your stewards to keep a watchful eye on the crowd and to inform the police of any untoward behaviour but not to get involved.

Drunks are also an unpleasant but inevitable result of any street event. You cannot restrict drinking in the street unless it is a designated 'dry area' as are some town centres in England, but you can prevent drinking on the floats. It is, of course, illegal to drive under the influence of alcohol, and though not illegal it is particularly dangerous to allow any other participant access to alcohol. Make it clear in the rules and at the public meeting that alcohol will not be tolerated and will result in instant disqualification from the competition and non-acceptance of an entry next year.

One event I was involved with entered a splendid and beautifully constructed float that towered into the sky. Half way down the route it became entangled in some low lying telephone or electricity cables. This goes to show that you must check the height of your route as well as the width and publish any restrictions in the rules.

You should ask each float to display three numbers, front, back and the near side so that stewards can immediately identify the floats if there is a problem. Numbers should not obscure the windscreen as it an offence to obscure the driver's vision. Ensure that children are supervised, and warn drivers to watch for pedestrians running between floats and to take special care negotiating corners and obstructions.

Collectors should walk beside the floats and go into the crowds. Spectators should be encouraged to stay where they are and not to run forwards to put money in buckets. Accidents have happened in the past with flying coins; if there are enough collectors this should be reduced. Make sure that people do not throw

Emergencies and safety checklist

- ❏ Minimise risk.
- ❏ Book Red Cross or St John Ambulance.
- ❏ Inform emergency services.
- ❏ Allow 'gateways' through barriers.
- ❏ Use fireworks safely.
- ❏ Ban alcohol on floats.
- ❏ Check overhead cables.
- ❏ Number each float.
- ❏ Use the rules to encourage safety aspects.
- ❏ Remember to extend the hours of car parks.

freebies off the floats. It encourages children to run into the road to pick things up with possibly fatal results. Each float should carry their own insurance and should only be accepted entry on production of a current certificate.

Make sure that you arrange for official car parks to be open until the end of the event. This will help keep cars off the streets until the very end, and you will save a lot of people from becoming over-heated when they discover that their cars have been locked in the multi-story car parks overnight.

Put yourself in the shoes of the public and the participants and you will have a very successful event.

Outside Concerts

EVENT 2
Outside Concerts

'The circus is coming to town!'. If you were born before the end of the fifties you might just remember the knot of excitement in your stomach at those words. Even quite small towns had their annual visit, but by the end of the sixties the travelling circus had all but died out except for the huge names that we still see on our television screens.

Something had to take its place, and in America that something was the Pop Festival. It wasn't long before the craze for outside events growing around the culture of popular music was taking off on this side of the Atlantic too. The Isle of Wight festival was an event that every parent dreaded and it certainly wasn't a family event in the way that the circus was.

However, there really is something unique about an activity that is usually held within the confines of a building being organised under temporary structures or even right out in the open.

The 'circus-coming-to-town' mentality, to quote Richard Abel, the site co-ordinator from the Glastonbury Festival, is still as exciting and real today as it was a hundred years ago. It takes a strong will to walk on past lines of lorries and trucks arriving piled high with equipment, scaffolding and brightly coloured tenting without stopping to stare. The town buzzes with talk and the activity is there in the centre of things for all to see. The potential for self-advertising is enormous and so is sponsorship if your choose your subject matter carefully.

Now, I'd like to make it plain right away that the likes of the re-run Woodstock, the Reading Festival or even Glastonbury itself are not for amateurs at the events game. Nor do I think that you should tackle 'overnighters' which can cause all sorts of extra problems which I will go into later. Crowds of 100,000, 50,000 or even 20,000 people are not for first-timers. However there is no reason why you should not aspire to the same atmosphere or aim for something exceptional albeit considerably reduced in size. New organisers should be able to handle a show of 6,000–

8,000 people, which is still a large scale event, especially if you have a co-operative local police force, buy a certain amount of expertise in, and are willing to take advice.

A successful event of this type raises money through ticket sales and sponsorship. You can also use other means to boost funds which we will look at in more detail later in the chapter.

Fundraisers for charitable organisations have further considerations above and beyond the basic profit margin concerns of all promoters. It is vitally important that your organisation is not seen to be associating itself with anything that could be construed as 'cult', 'shady' or even downright illegal. Apart from the bad PR, you will meet considerable resistance from the authorities. Music events are sometimes scenes of violence and alcohol or drug abuse, and it is imperative that these elements are addressed and eliminated as far as possible. Your choice of entertainment and your target market will go some way to dealing with this problem. Just to give you a very obvious example, an event promoted as a 'rave' to include groups playing Acid House is bound to have the police really hopping about, and even if you could get permission, would probably send out all the wrong messages for your charity. However, an evening of crooners in the Frank Sinatra and Bing Crosby style, whilst being so safe as to hardly get the local Bobby walking past the gates, may not get you the turnout you want either. On second thoughts I'm not sure anyone has ever tried an outdoor lounge singer concert – it just might be what everyone has been waiting for!

Seriously though, you really need to think through what draws the crowds and the money but also what draws added problems. Aim for something popular within a tried and tested format if you are really new to the work.

Leaving the difficult areas aside, there is still a wide menu to suit all tastes. Audiences over the years have enjoyed all sorts of popular entertainment including the more obvious Rock and Roll, Blue Grass, Jazz, Reggae, Country and Western and Folk as well as main stream Pop. Classical music has had a good airing in this format, as have one-off operatic enterprises; witness the success of the three tenors at the World Cup in Italy.

The new rock and roll, so they say, is comedy. And with this in mind perhaps the style to go for, if you are organising an event of this kind for the first time, is a mixed bag, that is to say integrate comic acts with the music. You can't please all of the people all of the time but at least you will be appealing to a broad base.

The thing to remember about comedy is that it is an intimate entertainment. It is hard to be intimate with 8,000 people, and only the seriously good can keep control of that number for two or three hours. American comedians, such as Richard Prior, are probably better at dealing with large audiences than comics from the UK. British comics are often understated, with perhaps only Billy Connelly showing the sort of presence with large crowds that is really necessary to sustain a whole evening. The seriously good go out for serious money and are probably unaffordable. Second-raters will really look second rate after an evening of unremitting comedy. But interspersed with music and a good continuity personality such as Jools Holland they will come good, and there is the basis of a really popular and highly entertaining event.

Ultimately, of course, what you put into your event is up to you. Your area may have some very talented local acts and bands that you can use and give a well deserved break. You may have a famous orchestra on your doorstep that is prepared to play in unconventional circumstances just for the fun of it or perhaps a choir that is particularly suited to the outdoor treatment. For the purposes of this book I will look at the comedy and music mix in detail, and you can pick the sections out that are relevant or make adjustments where necessary.

Before you start

Prior to leading you through the complexities of organising an outside music event you need to know that the (almost) definitive work already exists. 'The Guide to Health, Safety and Welfare at Pop Concerts and Similar Events' is an HMSO publication put together by the Health and Safety Commission, the Home Office and the Scottish Office. This book is clear, concise and thorough, and is the result of several experts pooling all their considerably wide experience. It is compulsory reading for anyone who is organising an outdoor concert. I am not in the business of re-inventing the wheel, so I intend to leave you to read and assimilate the relevant parts from this excellent guide for yourselves.

A detailed work on how to organise a musical event, however, is not enough for your needs. I hope that when you have read through this section, that you will also know why you are advised to do things a certain way and also how to dovetail technical and legal information with the unique and very particular needs of organising an event as a major fundraiser for a charitable organisation.

Therefore, I urge you to read this chapter in conjunction with the HMSO Guide and the other books detailed in the box on page 52.

**Three books you cannot be without
(details at the back of this book)**

1 *'The Guide to Health, Safety and Welfare at Pop Concerts and Similar Events'* – HMSO (colloquially known as the Pop Code).

2 *'Code of Practice for Outside Events'* – National Outdoor Events Association

3 *Organising Local Events'* – Directory of Social Change

Three books you may find helpful

4 *The White Book'* – Birdhurst Ltd

5 *Showcall'* – Stage and Television Today

6 *The Showman's Directory'* – Lance Publications

Getting Started

As with all the events outlined in this book, organising something at this level is too much for one person and you will have to gather a team together to help you. Whether you choose to operate democratically within the structure of a committee or to employ people, either on a professional or a voluntary basis is probably up to the organisation that you are working with. But you do need to have clearly defined areas of activity and someone at the head to pull the whole thing together.

Areas that need to be covered include someone:

1 In charge of the site itself and all the plant
2 To co-ordinate all safety issues
3 To organise the catering and concessions
4 To book the acts
5 To co-ordinate the marketing and sponsorship
6 To manage the ticket sales
7 To head this team (probably you), to be responsible for making sure that all the legal and safety requirements are met, and to control the budget.

We have established, for the sake of this book, that you want to promote an outdoor music/comedy event or something similar. There are three more elements that must become clear before you can proceed. You need

1 A date.
2 A venue.
3 A target market.

Choosing a date

The United Kingdom is made up of a bunch of cold and wet little islands. Some a lot colder and wetter than others. June to early September is really the only time of the year that can realistically be considered to possibly produce the kind of weather that is needed to hold an event outside.

At the beginning of this chapter I suggested that you should not consider any 'overnighters' or a two day event. The problems of any event are greatly exacerbated when you have to make arrangements for overnight accommodation. Very briefly, campsites have to be made available, extra catering and facilities all have to be on hand. And whilst the potential for greater audience numbers are undoubtedly maximised, the logistical difficulties, security (both personal and to property) and policing problems are just not worth the hassle. I have not done the sums but I have a suspicion that the extra costs involved could actually lose money for some events.

In Norwich we ran one or two two-day festivals each year. But by 1987 the problems of drunkenness, suspected drug dealing, noise, and camper vans that did not leave the site for a week or more after the end of the event, quite apart from the refuse problems, caused the council and the police to ban any event that was planned to go into a second day. Many other local authorities have followed suit. From a personal point of view they can be frightening, and can quite suddenly get out of control in a way which is unlikely to happen over the course of a single day.

Of course, all over the country festivals are organised that do go on for a weekend or more but these are managed by professionals with much experience and even they can be caught by surprise. Richard Abel tells a cautionary tale of a festival he went to in Ireland during 1994, where the audience were expected to camp overnight. 'The Irish don't camp,' he told me, 'but nobody realised until it was too late'. A very few people arrived complete with tents. Then the tents were stolen. Then the people who had stolen the tents first had them stolen from them, and so the sorry circle continued. Before long the site was in uproar. Not a situation, I would suggest, for the uninitiated.

Having said all that, you may find that the marquee and equipment hire is based on a three-day let, and that two days will cost you very little more than one day, if anything at all. This means that you can run the same programme again but over two days, thus doubling your ticket sales but obviating the need to provide overnight accommodation – as you will be selling the same show to different customers not a different show to the same customers. You could run a different show, appealing to a different audience, during the same day – a family show in the afternoon and a more specialised show for the evening, perhaps. But you could run into VAT problems here if the event is large enough, as you may find you fall foul of the concession on one-off fundraising. Be prepared, take professional advice.

Most big events take place at the weekend. It is no coincidence that Friday, Saturday and Sunday are the most popular days for any entertainment. Monday to Thursday nights will rarely produce the audience that you are looking for, and if you need a large audience from further afield you will need to build in travel time so Friday won't do and Sunday may be too late. For a first event, Saturday is the day.

Don't forget to check the calendar for possible clashes. If you can, check TV schedules and avoid national sporting fixtures. You will greatly reduce your audience if you choose the one Saturday afternoon that England are due to play the West Indies at Lords or for the final of Wimbledon. Contact the local Tourist Information Centre to find a good day and firm up your date at least nine to twelve months in advance if you can so that it can be included in all national listings.

What time? Well, I think we can safely eliminate the morning. We don't have a tradition of going out for entertainment before lunch in this country and the extra setting up time is always useful. The local authorities and the police would probably prefer you to stage your event in the early evening – starting at about 5.30pm, but that may not be possible. The restrictions of your Public Entertainments Licence will certainly dictate that you have to finish playing amplified music somewhere between 10.30pm and midnight if you are near a residential area.

Look at your prospective audience, and if you expect to appeal to the whole family an afternoon or early evening show is ideal. A bit more specialised or aiming at an older group and you would do better to consider traditional theatre times.

Choosing a date checklist

❏ Consider potential weather conditions.

❏ Think hard before deciding on a two-day event.

❏ Consider different shows at the same venue.

❏ Choose a weekend (probably).

❏ Check for rival events.

❏ Choose a time to suit your audience and the requirements of your licence.

Choosing a venue

The site for the event itself does not have to be as large as you might imagine. But you do need open spaces in the vicinity to provide for car parking, support vehicles and all the peripheral services. A good event site should be tight and logical with wide aisles to allow for smooth crowd movement. It is vital that it is not a 'closed' site with restricted access. Before you consider any venue you must check that the means of escape and emergency exits are adequate. Glastonbury covers a massive 600 acres, but even the largest events in Norwich are comfortably held within an 80-acre site.

Grass is ideal and provides a comfortable and kind surface to walk on when it is dry. If it is long you will have to arrange to get it cut and if it is wet the surface can be hazardous. The organisers at Glastonbury use motor bikes to get around the site, and this proved impossible after heavy rain; it's not too good for the elderly either. Wire-netting securely pegged into the ground at heavily used areas can save accidents and the surface. Jute mats are another option, but are really only good inside a tent. Remember also that whilst cars may be OK parking after rain, large lorries may have trouble getting out of a boggy site, especially if it is uphill. Part of one of the sites I used to use was near a river, and it never completely dried out. Horse boxes made a beeline for this area as it meant that the horses had water available nearby. Unfortunately, despite repeated warnings, there were often one or two vehicles that had to be towed out at the end of the day.

Grass is suitable for all temporary structures. Tar-macadam is good for some activities (e.g. car parking), but obviously, you cannot drive tent pegs into asphalt. Sand and dunes can be used but again watch out for vehicles getting stuck and be sensitive to possible erosion; there may be environmental implications. Sand is also hard work to get around on by foot after an hour or two.

Above all you need to choose a site that you can get to easily. A public park with good approach roads and integral car parking is probably as near to being perfect without actually finding a purpose built site. Most parks have drinking water on site, toilets and waste systems to enable you to install temporary WC blocks, and an electrical and gas supply. Many have three phase electricity available. If you choose a field in the middle of a farm you may well have to bring all utilities on site yourself which is certainly possible but greatly adds to the cost.

For a one-off event it is often an advantage to use a venue that is a traditional events site. It can take years to build up a reputation and it helps for the public to know exactly where they are going and know what to expect when they get there.

If you choose to use a council owned site read Chapter 5 in *'Organising Local Events'* which covers contacting the professionals and how to cut red tape. Local authority sites are often insured for you which can help keep costs down again.

Choosing a venue check list

❑ Include enough space for all the support services.

❑ Plan the site in a logical fashion and allow for ease of crowd movement.

❑ Check the emergency exits are adequate.

❑ Consider the suitability of the surface in all conditions.

❑ Consider access.

❑ Check on-site facilities.

❑ Look at the advantages of a 'traditional' or Council owned site.

Getting to know your target market

You might as well write your event off as a no-hoper here and now if you are not prepared to do a little research to find out if you have a market out there for your particular attraction.

It is true that any event being staged in an area for the first time is going to have an element of 'sticking your big toe into the water to see what it is like'. But there are quite a few areas that you can explore to either give you ideas as to what sort of entertainment you might put on or whether your ideas will work.

Firstly, look at what sells at the local theatres, even which genre goes down best in the cinemas. If you have a local college, art school or university, talk to the Students Union to get their opinion. Secondly, study the local press, especially the contemporary music columns to find out which comedians and local bands are popular. Thirdly, go to see your planned acts in action and see the sort of crowds that they draw. Finally, employ a good agency to advise and book the acts for you if you are at all worried about how to get hold of the people that you want or whether you are getting the right mix for your area, (see the section on Booking your Acts later in this chapter).

Many areas have a local publication, perhaps a *What's On* guide or a preview magazine, these can often provide more information and may be a good vehicle to carry advertising at a later date especially for events aimed at the 18-25s market.

It might be sensible at this point to remind you that an event which you are planning as a one-off and where tickets sales are your main fundraiser must have a built in 'Go no further' option. If, after doing your research you decide that there just isn't a market out there, throw in the towel and opt for some other type of event. If you have got further down the line and you are starting to sell tickets, but sales are pathetic and there is no reason why they should pick up, then you need to re-assess your position before it is too late. You may already have spent money, you may have a penalty clause to honour on the acts or the hire of equipment, but if you know that you are just going to lose more money on the night then it may be better to cut your losses and cancel.

When you design your planning schedule, build in a meeting two or three weeks before the event for this very purpose. It might be embarrassing and you might feel an almighty failure, but no-one will blame you if you try and save what money you can by calling a halt. It is far more likely that you will be vilified, especially by the press, and dragged over the coals if you proceed with an event where all the signs have told you to give up *(see section on Cancelling)*.

It is probably impossible to work down through your list of elements and cross off idea, date, venue, audience in nice easy stages. This part of the planning process is a juggling act and don't worry if you feel that all the balls are in the air at once. This is how it should be, and you would be unwise to firm up on any one element until you feel that you are happy with all aspects, at least in principle.

> **Target market check list**
>
> ❏ Research your market.
>
> ❏ Study local provision.
>
> ❏ Consider using an agency to book acts or even put the whole show together for you.
>
> ❏ Don't be afraid to cancel if necessary.

Site design and infrastructure

Your next task will be to start to design your site and work out and book the infrastructure. With today's advanced technology providing us with almost unlimited temporary structures, your problem is going to be one of choice. In a permanent structure you are forced by the building to choose certain options, outdoors you have a clean sheet. So let's look at some of your options. Your decision, in part, will be dictated by the way in which you choose to sell your tickets or, to look at it another way, the way you choose to sell your tickets will be dictated by how you fence the space.

Outside events can operate on two levels. You can work on the Disney Theme Park system where you make a charge for entering the site and everything else is free apart for some specialist activities, or you can operate the Fairground system which allows the public onto the site free of charge and every activity is separately priced. The main attractions are usually under cover and quite possibly seated; tickets can be bought in advance or on the door.

Fencing options
1. Security fence the whole site (site charge).
2. Part fence the perimeter to encourage crowd control (tickets only to main tents).
3. Fence an internal area and erect canvas barriers to prevent sight lines to the main entertainment (tickets only to central area).
4. Fence nothing (tickets at main tent).

Option 1 is only really possible if you can be sure of your fencing and you have very tight security. The opportunity for non-ticket holders gaining entry is enormous despite the 2-metre high mesh fencing that is now available.

Option 4 also has its disadvantages. If you can't adequately fence off the site, you may not be able to manage your crowd safely in the event of an emergency. There is free access for 'undesirables' and criminals can vanish with ease.

Personally the question of 'to fence or not to fence' was always my biggest headache. Look at your potential audience and decide if they really need serious control. If there is free access onto residential areas, you may need to fence certain parts of the perimeter to prevent damage to gardens or property.

Venue options

1 No formal structure. Raised staging and flown lighting rigs – covered. A pit area and main viewing area – uncovered. No seating
2 Contained area with or without seating. As above but with fencing and canvas sight line barriers.
3 Large clear span tent, no seats.
4 Clear span tent complete with seating.

Option 1 offers you a traditional pop festival style venue. There is freedom of movement for the crowd but it is open to the elements and crowd control is difficult. Of all the options this is the one for which you can sell the most tickets. An open event like this needs experienced and confident stewarding to prevent crowd surges. It is not suitable for an event at which children are present.

Option 2 is suitable for a more controlled concert. I have seen this work very well for classical concerts. It is also possible to provide seating for part of the area. The back can be a space as large as you like for standing room only. In practice people bring rugs to sit on, children in pushchairs are easily accommodated as are people using wheelchairs. If the staging is 2 metres or more high this will greatly add to the enjoyment of the crowd in the rear area. Classical music accompanied by a laser show is very spectacular held under a night sky if you can risk the possibility of a downpour. If you go for the no seating option and are presenting dance music then, again, professional stewards are needed.

Option 3 is good for a traditional contemporary music concert style and, with the addition of a properly constructed dance floor, this type of venue is very suitable for dance music. It offers maximum ticket sales in a venue that protects the public from the weather. It is not suitable for certain types of music that have particular appeal to people under 16 as mass hysteria is most likely within this age group. As in Option 1, you may need very careful stewarding.

The 'Pit' is situated between the front barriers and the stage (to stop the crowd gaining access to the stage itself). It is often slightly raised so that people can be lifted over the barrier more easily and to enable paramedics or stewards to have a clear sight of the audience.

Option 4 offers the best crowd control and is suitable for family events. However, a seated venue will reduce the amount of tickets that you can sell.

For first-time organisers the temporary building system has many advantages. Firstly, you can hire the venue complete with seats, floor, staging and satellite dressing rooms; some even come complete with a management and back stage crew to operate lighting and sound systems as an entire package. There is little need for costly perimeter fencing and a significant reduction in security personal requirements which can offset costs.

Secondly, the new EC laws, CEN (European Committee for Standardisation) standards and the government Pop Code have imposed such stringent restrictions on outdoor entertainment in the last few years that it is well worth the extra money of hiring in the whole caboodle to ensure that you present a professional, polished and above all legal show that is built to full European safety standards.

Thirdly, a tented structure can offer a full blackout, if necessary, that you cannot otherwise achieve until very late at night in June and July. 'Seating only' ensures that the fire regulation numbers are adhered to and shows up any fraudulent ticket schemes before it is too late.

And lastly, and perhaps most important of all, the audience are kept warm and dry whatever the weather conditions are outside, thereby ensuring you maximum sales during even the most unkind of British summers.

Of course there are disadvantages too, the major consideration being that of safety. A tented, solid walled, fully seated venue can be much slower to evacuate in an emergency than an open field and correspondingly, as stated above, the numbers you are allowed inside are reduced. Fire is a greater hazard but the up side is that crowd control is tighter.

Many temporary structures are licensed for up to 6,000 people, so you needn't cut your audience potential by much in choosing to operate all the main activities under cover.

Site design and infrastructure checklist

- ❑ Consider the age group of your audience.
- ❑ Look at potential hazards of neighbouring areas.
- ❑ Decide if you need seating.
- ❑ Look at all the opportunities for fencing as dictated by the site.
- ❑ Decide the most appropriate system for charging and design your site accordingly.
- ❑ Always put the safety of your audience and other personnel as your main priority.
- ❑ Remember to include families and people who have disabilities in your equations.
- ❑ Decide if you need a full blackout.
- ❑ Seriously consider employing a professional crew complete with equipment when you hire your tent or staging.

I strongly recommend that you go for a system that provides you with a complete 'package' with all the experience and advice that goes with it. The structure should hold a current fire licence, be built to the correct standards and satisfy all the regulations.

Roughing a site plan

So, lets assume that you have one main tent with ticket only entertainment happening over the course of an afternoon and evening in a council owned park offering basic utilities. You can start to rough out your basic design by working through in your head, or by using sketches, how the traffic (both vehicular and pedestrian) can flow.

Imagine that you are a family of four and are arriving by car.

1. You will need to reach the site from any direction reasonably easily *(signage)*.
2. At the approach you will expect to be able to see exactly where the car parks are and how much it costs to park *(stewards signs and arrows)*.
3. You drive your car into a car park that should not be more than five, or at the absolute outside, ten minutes walk from the main entrance. You are greeted by someone at the car park entrance who is able to take your money and give you change *(car park attendant)*.
4. Having left your car you will want to make your way over reasonable terrain towards the main gates avoiding being run over by more cars as you go *(pedestrian protection)*.
5. At the site entrance the opportunity to buy a site plan and a programme is useful. A large painted board depicting the site might also be an option *(site plans)*.
6. At this stage you notice an exhibition and enquiry stand showing the work of the benefiting charity *(information stand)*.
7. You may have already purchased a ticket for the main entertainment in advance but if you haven't you will want to find a ticket office *(ticket booth)*.
8. The ticket booth will be near the main tent which is probably situated in the centre of the site but against one boundary if possible, to provide a natural secure area for crew trucks and support vehicles *(main structure)*.
9. If your children are like mine, they will already be clamouring that they are hungry so you will move to the end of the site where there are food concessions *(drinking water, electricity or generators, skip for rubbish, safe area for LPG bottles)*.

10. These concessions will be placed in a group around a beer tent and a separate soft drinks bar. Behind these tents is a service road for bowsers and deliveries *(concessions and bars)*.

11. There may be a dedicated picnic area where you can eat your food without being mown down by the crowds *(picnic area)*.

12. And you will need plenty of litter bins to be readily available *(refuse facilities)*.

13. The trek to the food area takes you past other entertainments including perhaps a small tent offering circus skills to young children, a mobile creche, trade stands and promotional material for the bands *(peripheral activities)*.

14. In due course the family will need to use the toilet facilities and these are arranged in three or more blocks around the outside of the site so that they can be serviced from the back *(toilets)*.

15. Near the centre of the site, sporting a large flag and a public address system *(PA)* is the event office *(site office)*. This could be part of the ticket office.

16. The First Aid office is here too *(first aid)*.

17. You are booked into the last performance and emerge from the tent well after dark and will need to see where you are going *(floodlights)*.

18. The main aisle is wide enough to allow most of the audience to move quickly towards the car park or other approach roads, although other activities may carry on for an hour or so more.

19. Back in the floodlit car park, the traffic which has been carefully controlled to exit down a separate route away from the entrance during the day is now allowed to leave from the entrances also, to allow a swift evacuation.

It may seem a bit pedestrian to think of an event in this way, and experienced site designers do not need to go through these processes. But by sketching things through in your head like this, you can try out all sorts of possibilities before you firm up on anything. You need to have a very clear idea in your own mind what it is that you want from your event and how it is to 'feel', and it helps to put yourself in the shoes of the type of audience that you are hoping to attract. I have given you an example of what comes out of my head, but you may have very different ideas. Talk them through with the professionals who are supplying the main structure and take their advice. Talk, also, to the council's Events Promotion Officer if you are using a local authority park; she or he will have seen many events through on that site and can advise you as to any quirks or problems that might be peculiar to the site.

Make a list, as I have done, of anything that strikes you as you work your way along the event's path. In *'Organising Local Events'* you will find a basic checklist to ensure that you don't forget anything major.

> Remember: safety of personnel – crowd, crew, entertainers, stewards, everyone – is your number one priority.

Safety

This imaginary exercise will only assist in designing a layout from the audience point of view, which may not be the same as a management view point. When you have got your perfect site, or so you think, it is useful to run the whole process through again, but this time in the emergency services' shoes. And again as though you were back stage. And again as a trader, and so on. Of course, safety is paramount and if you have to compromise comfort for safety or ease of back stage access for safety or the needs of traders for safety then safety should win every time.

There are a number of situations that can constitute an emergency.

1. Fire.
2. Crowd 'collapse'.
3. Structure collapse.
4. Power failure.
5. Flood.

Fire

Fire is the nightmare of all event organisers and can occur at the smallest events. You will be employing large amounts of electrical equipment in temporary buildings. There are very likely to be cooking facilities dotted around the site, there may well be LPG heating, petrol driven vehicles and people who smoke cigarettes. Quite apart from what you have brought to the site there are probably several fire hazards already in the area including dried grass, overhanging trees, and wooden buildings.

You must read Part III of the *Pop Code* thoroughly to familiarize yourself with all the requirements. You must inform all the stewards and back stage personnel of emergency procedures and provide adequate fire fighting equipment, which can be hired from specialist companies. You will also need to arrange training in the equipment use. You must ensure that you have provided enough emergency exits in crowd control barriers and in fencing at regular intervals to ensure quick evacuation for the expected numbers. You will not be granted a Public

Entertainments Licence until you can satisfy the authorities that you are complying with the recommendations.

If you are worried that you cannot fulfil the requirements you should ask for advice from a Health and Safety Officer or the Fire Officer for your area. It is probably good practice to invite one or more members of the emergency services to be part of the planning team anyway.

It is unlikely that you will encounter bomb threats, real or otherwise at an event of this type, but it is as well to keep in mind that your benefiting charity may have opposition. You should prepare a policy and procedure if the unthinkable does happen.

Crowd collapse

Crowd 'collapse' is a situation where the surge forward towards the stage is so sudden or so powerful that the front rows of the crowd cannot support the pressure from behind, and fall to the ground running considerable risk of crushing or asphyxiation. At this point the situation is very hard to rectify and the only option is for the performers to stop their stage act and assume control. Young or inexperienced acts sometimes do not realise what a huge responsibility they have in controlling the audience, and it is your job to advise them of signals that will alert them to this situation and what you want them to do on their part.

Crowd surges happen most often within a crowd that includes a high proportion of young teenagers and care must be taken when organising an event which appeals to this market; serious thought must be given to making it all seated. If you feel that this will greatly reduce the enjoyment of the audience then you must take advice from the HSE (Health and Safety Executive).

In one rock venue where I worked the capacity was only 1,500 people, but we still experienced worrying crowd behaviour. An effective solution was to install crowd control barriers across an area in front of the stage and 'pit' (known as the cattle pen) in lines allowing just ten rows of people between each one. This had the added advantage of allowing two or three sections to be barrier-ed off whenever we had to accommodate TV cameras, which was fairly often as we hosted the BBC Sight and Sound Concerts on a regular basis. As the crowd moved forward the pressure was never allowed to build up because the barriers took the strain. A natural corridor formed in front of each row facilitating the movement of staff. Stewards are necessary to prevent people climbing the barriers at the beginning of the show, and it is important that barriers are of the correct height and have sufficient strength and rigidity to avoid buckling or movement and becoming an additional hazard in themselves. (Detailed barrier information is given in the Pop Guide.)

Structure collapse

Structure collapse is, mercifully, very rare and is almost always entirely due to misuse. Towers or stacks of sound equipment have been known to be pulled off stage or fall off when people try and climb up them so stage barriers must be carefully constructed. Even seated audiences can start such a 'crowd sway' that the structures are put under extraordinary loading causing whole sections to collapse. Again the way to deal with such crowd behaviour is to control it from the stage, and the performers have a responsibility to ensure that swaying does not get out of hand. Remember too that high winds can cause structure damage.

Power failure

Power failure can be quite catastrophic during a very large and popular concert. It used to be the very unwise practice for Environmental Health Inspectors to 'pull the plug' on a band that was continually flouting the decibel level ratings for a particular venue resulting in an immediate riot from the audience. A genuine power failure can have the same effect if you are not prepared.

Back-up equipment is vital. For a smaller scale event this may only necessitate an adequate public address system and emergency lighting so that you can explain the situation and beg forgiveness for a delay or to evacuate people. At a larger event you may need a total back-up so that you can continue with the show as if nothing had happened. It goes without saying that an installation should be so designed as to avoid any tampering from members of the public or, indeed, any other unauthorised person. A suitable electrical certificate will need to be produced as part of the requirements of the Public Entertainments Licence; more details of this later.

Safety check list

❏ Read part III of the *Pop Code* thoroughly.

❏ Check site for fire hazards both before you set up and after.

❏ Plan your emergency procedures carefully and train the crew. Run a drill through until you are satisfied.

❏ Hire the correct fire fighting equipment and train operators.

❏ Arrange for a signal to be given to the stage act that informs them of crowd problems.

❏ Take advice from the HSE in all aspect of safety.

❏ Ensure that the audience cannot reach equipment on stage or the sound and lighting desks.

❏ Arrange for back-up power and emergency lighting if necessary.

❏ Decide on a Plan B in the event of exceptional weather conditions both for the event itself or for potential evacuations.

Flood

Flood is very unlikely, but if you are organising a large event beside the sea or other expanse of water it may be a consideration. Alternatively excessive rainfall may not directly effect the event itself in producing an immediate crisis unless it is to be held largely in the open air, but it could cause extreme difficulties in rendering the ground totally unsuitable for evacuating the crowd. Care must be taken in choosing a space that is not subject to regular flooding, and car parks should sited on reasonably firm terrain wherever possible. Extraordinary weather conditions could cause a power failure or make structures unsafe. You need to know when and how an event should be cancelled on grounds of safety. See 'Cancelling a show' at the end of this chapter.

Other venue facilities

Apart from the main tent, already discussed above, all the infrastructure that you might need is also detailed in *'Organising Local Events'* and you should perhaps read Chapters 7, 9, 10 and 19 through to familiarise yourself with what is needed and where you can get it from. Make sure that you are absolutely sure what is required by law according to the *Pop Code* and that you are following guidelines to the letter.

In my opinion, having got your main structures complete with staging and safety features in place, the next most important feature of any outside event are the drinking water and toilet facilities. These can make or break an event for some people and many are frankly, truly 'Ugh!'. Even if your chosen site has WC facilities available, you will have to hire many more in. Place lavatories in groups around the outside of the site, apart from a block for wheelchair users and/or a baby-change facility if you are expecting to attract whole families, which should be more accessible.

Freely available drinking water is not usually needed at an event that has seated accommodation and where people are not expected to attend for more than a few hours. However, if conditions are hot and cramped and a dance floor is provided, you must make provision for a plentiful supply of clean drinking water.

Second only to the loos in importance of 'site hygiene' is the way in which you deal with rubbish. Empty oil drums are better than tuff-tubs as they are less likely to roll about in the wind, do not present a fire hazard, have a greater capacity and are unattractive enough not to go 'walkabout' – which, believe it or not, is a problem that I have experienced. Arrange them in groups, especially near the food concessions and toilet blocks, and furnish each group with a pole garnished with a flag on the top so they can be seen through even the densest crowd. If the event is expected to last more than a few hours you will have to make arrangements to empty them. In windy weather you will have to empty bins more often as litter blows out of containers more than two thirds full. So make sure that you supply enough containers.

Other facilities check list

❏ If you are a first time organiser, read the relevant chapters in the other books in this series.

❏ Ensure that you have an adequate quality and quantity of WCs.

❏ Ensure you provide adequate drinking water where necessary.

❏ Provide enough litter bins and sign them clearly.

The importance of considering less able people

I have already briefly mentioned wheelchair users, but I think a more detailed statement may be useful. Don't forget that people with walking, hearing and seeing difficulties can and should be able to enjoy a large outdoor event. With just a little consideration from the site designer their opportunity for enjoyment is greatly enhanced.

A loop system for people with impaired hearing is not difficult to install into a seated auditorium, and specialist firms should be able to advise you if your hired-in venue management team do not supply a loop themselves.

A registered blind person should be able to bring an assistant in to the auditorium free of charge as should someone who has to use a wheelchair.

Simon Barnes from the International Spinal Research Trust suggests that you imagine that you are pushing a fully loaded wheel barrow around a site to get the idea of what it is like to have to propel a wheelchair over grass or gravel. If you think you could push a wheelbarrow comfortably between the disabled car park to the venue and the toilets without having to negotiate

---

Less able needs checklist

❏ Consider installing a loop system.

❏ Advertise that wheelchair users and visually impaired people can bring a helper free of charge.

❏ Think about exits, entrances, ticket outlets, seating and evacuation in terms of the less able.

steps, steep slopes or boggy ground, then you have got things about right. If not, well perhaps you should think again. Incidentally pushing a toddler in a pushchair meets many of the same requirements, and if you get things right for one you may well improve matters for the other.

Security

Even a few years ago crime on an events site was restricted to a few fights, the odd pickpocket and some alcohol abuse. I could walk around a big rural site in perfect safety, even carrying cash, suffering only verbal abuse from time to time and rarely feeling threatened. One of the un-lovelier trends of outside events in recent times is the emergence of the more serious face of crime. Fraud can be a big problem, especially if you are selling tickets in advance. Robbery – both of cash and produce – from trader's stands has reached epidemic proportions. Drug dealing at certain events is endemic. And violence, especially where money is concerned, is also a distinct possibility on city centre sites in some regions.

The provision of a safe, controlled event has to be weighed against making the whole thing so antiseptic as to have bleached out the unique atmosphere that you should be striving to create. Keeping the ticket price down helps – about £5 or £6 should be your top limit (unless you plan a classical music event); there is less to be gained from a complicated ticket scam. Booking less exciting but more middle-of-the-road entertainment also controls the type of audience you can expect and offering a family environment can help keep the atmosphere a bit more laid back but this may be moving away from the central idea.

Selling alcohol by the glass (or plastic cup) in a restricted area also dissuades under age drinking and prevents tins from being passed around the site. You might try to restrict alcohol from being brought onto the site or supplied other than from licensed tents; but from experience, this is very hard to enforce. The police may insist on certain restrictions before the recommendation for a Liquor Licence is put through, and you should work hard to deal with their concerns. Frankly, no alcohol can mean disaster and a dry show is no crowd-puller.

One of the problems with choosing not to supply a perimeter fence is one of protection of property during the setting up time. The tent will arrive at least 24 hours before time, and quite possibly well before then if you hire a large one, especially if you are putting complicated sound and lighting systems into

Security checklist

❑ Look realistically at areas where crime might present a problem.

❑ Try to eradicate temptation.

❑ Consider altering the atmosphere to make your event less threatening and encourage more family entertainment.

❑ Look at the way you sell alcohol.

❑ Make arrangements to protect equipment outside show times.

it. You will have to provide professional security, particularly during the hours of darkness. In truth, even if your site is fenced, you will still have to provide security as people always manage to climb in or enter through the fire exits anyway. The crew will sleep on site and protect their equipment up to a point, but you need to be aware of potential problems.

Marketing and sponsorship

If you are going to make any money out of an event like this sponsorship is vital. In fact if you do not attract a major sponsor towards the beginning of your planning, it may not be worth going ahead with the event at all.

Raising funding for a once-only event is very energy and time consuming. You need to be professional and resilient. Glastonbury operated at a loss for seven years before it finally became the charitable money-spinner that it is today. (Michael Eavis guarantees a quarter of a million pounds for charitable organisations before he checks his profits.) Sponsors really do like to see an event in action before they make up their minds, and if you have never attempted an event on this scale before they will be understandably nervous about linking their company name with a potential pup. Show that you are responsible and that your standards are high by preparing your proposal very carefully. Don't 'scatter gun' the market. Aim your proposal very precisely at one company, and show that you understand their needs by doing some research first.

Try to raise as much from one source as you can. It is a rare event that can support two major sponsors without the objectives becoming blurred. Sponsorship is far too big a subject to give it anything but a cursory mention here, but there are some excellent books on the subject and there are details of several publications at the back of this book.

Look at your event with a critical eye and put yourself in the position of potential sponsoring companies. You need to give them ample opportunities to benefit. It might help to read through the chapter by Mick Bennett of Sport for Television on Raising

Company Sponsorship in *'Tried and Tested Ways of Raising Money Locally'.*

Keep in mind that apart from wanting to sell more of their products or services companies may also be looking for an opportunity to launch a new image, change direction, develop a different customer profile, break into a new region, publicise a particular campaign or popularise a new personality.

A great opportunity that springs to mind is the imminent privatisation of the railways. Just think of all those new companies that need good PR! They may have car parks or delivery yards that would make perfect sites too. Certainly if you could find a park or field alongside the line you would have a good potential for publicity. Just look at how the Reading Festival announces itself by building a festival venue alongside one of the busiest commuter lines in the South of England. Personally I've always wanted to use a whole main line terminus for a day, I think the acoustics would be mind-blowing!

The most obvious sponsor to go for is a drinks company. Heineken already sponsor a travelling tent but you might find a local brewery who would welcome the possibility of sponsoring something locally. Other areas to look are insurance, electricity companies, specialist magazines or papers (e.g. NME – New

---

Opportunities for the sponsor

There are many opportunities that you can offer your sponsor. You can:

- Include the company name on all stationery, publicity, tickets, programmes and promotional material. Be careful about including the name in the title of the event unless you really cannot guarantee sponsorship in any other way.
- Provide free tickets and a VIP car parking area.
- Provide a company VIP hospitality tent and back stage tours with a possibility of meeting the 'stars'.
- Fly banners and flags showing the company logo.
- Use the company colours in special areas.
- Dedicate the main tent or area to the company.
- Include the company in a press conference to launch the partnership and afterwards organise an official handing over of monies and declaration of the funds raised for the charity at the end.
- Allow the company chairman to make a quick speech, perhaps about the work of your charity, before the show.
- Offer active involvement in preparing press releases.
- Allow the company a free trade stand.

Musical Express), local newspaper companies (vital for discount advertising), the local council, or, if you have something very unique to offer, TV production companies.

Listen to what the company requires from the event but remember that you also have a valuable commodity and that is the reputation of your charity. Do not compromise the organisation, and don't let the sponsoring company run away with linking their name to yours unless you are absolutely sure that you both are benefiting.

Carry your professionalism through until after the event by preparing a full package of photographs, press cuttings, thank you letters, reports and other evidence, to show them that they have benefited from supporting your event and they will be more likely to help you another time.

If you think you can persuade your headliner act to stay for an after-the-show party, you may be able to offer an opportunity for the sponsors to meet people involved in the show. This is particularly important if your sponsor has paid for the appearance fees.

When you have attracted your major sponsor, you may be able to work in tandem with their own PR company to work out a marketing plan. They may have special dates or launches that they need to build in and you can be guided by their experience. But again, don't compromise the charity. Your needs are paramount and you need to make sure that your own requirements are met. This event is your one opportunity to make a grand splash. Don't waste it.

If you are not attracting the amount of sponsorship that you need you might be able to approach the funding problem from a different angle. Service and equipment suppliers are beginning to appreciate the difficulties that organisers have in attracting sponsorship for one-off events. They recognise that unless organisations gain funding they will not be able to afford the expensive equipment that is required by law, and their own supply company will founder. In response to this problem suppliers have taken to offering equipment and a sponsor together as a package. One supplier I spoke to suggested this was a growing trend so, increasingly, you should be able to find tenting, crowd control equipment and other necessities available at a discounted price – provided, of course, that you and your major sponsor are prepared to put up with the inevitable advertising that will be carried on individual items.

Whilst a charity benefit can have very different objectives to a straight commercial operation it is no different when it comes to marketing the event itself. All events need an audience, preferably as big as you can manage and to achieve that you need to publicise.

Use every marketing tool that you can, even employ a good, reasonably priced public relations professional if you think you need help (but expect to pay around £200 a working day for one).

Plan a marketing schedule fairly early on and try to exploit the marketing potential of other key points in the charities own PR campaign. For instance if you are employing a new appeals manager, link in the forthcoming event. If a crisis has occurred where your organisation has been drafted in to provide short term relief, make sure you publicise the show at every opportunity. Once you have the event up and running use it as a PR tool as well as a way of raising money.

Consider all the obvious ways of marketing your event; press releases, interviews for the radio, advertising in the press, on posters, on the radio, on banners across the street, on Teletext or Oracle, in the tourism listings or at other events. Be creative and try a few less obvious routes; run a few pre-event events with buskers in the street, abseil down a public building with a banner, use sandwich boards, give away balloons, make advertising bookmarks and ask the local book shops or the library to put them in customers' books, try to arrange an interview on local television.

Match your marketing to your sponsor. A brewery might be very happy for you to 'gate-crash' pubs and hand out leaflets or advertise on beer mats. A motor company might supply a vehicle to drive about the area carrying bill boards or announce the event through a public address system (you may have to get permission).

On the whole it is probably better to advertise the event for the event's sake rather than as an opportunity to support a certain cause. By all means

---

Marketing and Sponsorship checklist

❏ If you are trying a new format, be aware that you may have to run an event several times before you make serious money.

❏ Prepare a professional proposal for sponsors and aim at one major source if possible.

❏ Consider what you can offer them in return for their support.

❏ Consider how you can make privatisation work for you.

❏ Do not compromise the charity.

❏ Prepare a post-event package.

❏ Use the company's PR team to help you if you can.

❏ If you fail to attract one large sponsor, put together easily saleable offerings for several companies.

❏ Look for equipment companies that include sponsorship.

❏ Plan a realistic marketing schedule.

❏ Stress the work of the charity less powerfully as you near the date of the event.

❏ Use appropriate marketing tools but consider anything, however weird.

publicise the shock, horror stories in the initial press releases and show what is to be achieved with the £10,000 you hope to raise; you might receive some donations then and there and at least you will encourage people to make a date in their diaries. As the date draws near tone down the charity connection and major on the entertainment value and, if you can, the value for money side. Do stress any volunteer help for the charity. Encourage stewards or other volunteers to wear charity tabards on the day. The public will like to feel that they are not paying for all the personnel that they see on the site and it helps to make volunteers feel important and part of an elite team as well as providing the obvious visibility advantage.

Maximising potential

Your major income will be raised from ticket sales. Hopefully you will have raised enough sponsorship to pay for the main tent. Any extra income is all to the good and can go towards paying for bigger names or straight into the profit margin.

There are plenty of opportunities to sell advertising space for a start. If you make your programme glossy and colourful, carrying some interesting articles you should have no trouble in selling advertisements. Advance tickets can be sold in a folder covered in advertising blocks and you can sell space on the reverse of the ticket itself – a local McDonalds is often a successful choice. Site plan leaflets can carry advertising, allowing you to give them away free of charge and if you choose to use boards, these too can be surrounded by advertising space.

Special promo beer mats could carry an advertisement on one side and the event logo on the other. Who knows, if these are specially attractive and carry a date and year, they could become collectors' items in years to come.

There is a complete warehouse of ideas for promotional material and merchandising. No doubt the charity will have its own collection of badges, balloons, gifts and T-shirts but you can add some unique to the event. There may be certain items that lend themselves to being overprinted, thus reducing your overheads. T-shirts and sweat shirts can be printed on the back and badges, pens, hats and bags are all relatively cheap to produce. There are also companies who specialise in organising mass balloon releases, providing yet another way of raising money. Perhaps a word about balloon releases might be appropriate here. In America there have been so many events of this type that they have experienced environmental pollution due to plastic waste. The balloons drift away and eventually rupture or just come down on the ground or in the water and birds and animals eat them with fatal consequences. There are now biodegradable balloons available which might be worth insisting on.

If you include a lucky number on the programme and hold a draw at the end of the show for a sponsored prize, you can add to your programme sales; but make sure you publicise it well. A person to person collection on the site and perhaps within the tent itself can help boost funds but you need to decide if these extra ideas detract from the atmosphere of the event that you wish to create.

If the entrance to the site is free, you may wish to charge for car-parking. Judy Weeks from Performing Arts Management, a company dealing solely in classical concerts in the grounds of stately homes, suggests to all her clients that they employ a professional car parking team – 'efficient access and exit can make or break the evening'. I am sure this is true of classical concerts where you can reasonably expect a large proportion of older middle-class people all arriving by car, but I am not so convinced for popular or even jazz concerts especially if people can be expected to leave at different times. Car parking must not be a shambles but experienced volunteers can be very good.

Chapter 10 in *Organising Local Events* will give you all the details you need on making it pay and how to set out your car park. If you do not have enough volunteers from your charity to steward the car park you may find the local Lions Club more than willing to step into the breach. Negotiate a flat fee with them to be paid to you for the privilege, and they can keep the money that they make on the gate to give to the charity of their choice. If you are lucky, it just might be yours!

The fact that you have a main tent doesn't preclude you from having all sorts of other activities supporting the main event and if you make the other entertainment interesting and exciting you will boost your attendance figures as long as you include them in your publicity. Other distinctly defined activities provide an opportunity to attract other minor sponsors who will welcome the chance to have their company name kept separate from that of the main sponsors.

Maximising potential checklist

❏ Sell advertising space.

❏ Sell promotional material and merchandising.

❏ Consider a balloon release.

❏ Include a raffle for programme numbers.

❏ Consider charging for car parking.

❏ Consider support entertainment.

Catering and concessions

It greatly adds to your organisational responsibilities and worries if you decide to run the catering and bars yourself. The easiest way to manage things is to offer all the main catering out to tender and invite applications for pitches for fast food and other trade stands.

However, it is greatly to your financial advantage if you keep control of the bar. Income from bar sales is not to be sneezed at and will considerably swell your funds. For a one-day event you may not feel that you need a major catering tent in any case and small concessions may fill the gap very nicely. Of course, if your major sponsor is a drinks company or a brewery the bar may be taken out of your hands anyway.

For ordinary trade stands you will need to advertise in the local press about 4-6 months in advance. Your pitch fee should be adjusted to the number of hours that you will be operating and the expected crowd figures. Fees will vary from region to region and you will need to do some research to find the right price to charge. For an all-day event where you will see 8,000-10,000 people it would not be unreasonable to charge a top price of £200 or £300, at an evening only event in the North of England £25 might be your limit. You need to think about discounts for charity stands and perhaps a double rate for anything over a certain square footage. If you are offering corporate hospitality opportunities in the main tent – perhaps at a classical concert – you can think along more extravagant lines.

More and more outside events these days include a fairground alongside. You do need to be careful that you are not turning your event into a 'rave', but a carefully chosen and sited fairground can do much to enhance the atmosphere. Consider a Victorian theme with steam driven carousels, swing boats and candy floss stalls, or perhaps a children's fun fair might be the option to go for during the day. Fairground organs are also very popular as long as they don't compete with what is going on in your main tent.

Catering concessions checklist

❑ Invite tenders for the main concessions.

❑ Consider keeping control of the bars.

❑ Offer corporate hospitality.

❑ Consider all the implications of adding a fair ground.

❑ Think about how external noise can affect your main attraction.

Ticket sales

Tickets should be made available in advance. Let the tickets go on sale at least a month before the show and possibly a lot longer than that. Provide a city or town centre box office if possible. A caravan in a pedestrian precinct will do, but if your charity or the major sponsor has a centrally placed office or store, a desk just inside the door is ideal. Some Tourist Information Centres will handle advance sales, on commission and some towns have a central 'ticket shop'. A credit card facility is also desirable enabling you to run an advance sales telephone line, and a postal address is vital.

If you are a one-off promoter all the above might seem rather daunting, and it can cost several hundreds of pounds to arrange extra telephone lines and staff to handle the advance bookings of a popular large-scale show, quite apart from training staff to cope with the on-site box office requirements.

A modern and effective way out of these problems is to employ a professional advance box-office service. An advance sales telephone number and address encouraging credit card use is advertised on all publicity. All sales are handled by computer at a remote office using trained staff and effective cash handling procedures. On the day the company arrive, complete with temporary box offices, computers and staff to use on site. They handle the cash and security and you do not have to worry about anything apart from picking up the cheque, less their costs, at the end. This method is highly recommended. The extra costs involved can be balanced by the saving on hiring in your own equipment, staff and training, all of which can be very costly for a one-off show.

Make sure that the on site box office is kept away from the entrance to the main tent or from the site entrance if you are charging a site charge. In my experience a multi-windowed box office set aside from the main entrances can greatly assist in reducing queues and over crowding. At some events it may be necessary to search members of the audience before they gain entry and if this can be separated from the ticket sales, so much the better.

Ticket sales checklist

❏ Sell tickets in advance.

❏ Provide a town centre box office or at least a credit card facility over the telephone.

❏ Consider employing a professional box-office service.

❏ Use multi-windowed box-offices on site to reduce queues.

··

Pricing

Do not assume that you will have a full house. I have always worked to very conservative figures of 50% capacity for an indoor show and 40% for an outdoor event. For a very large scale event with a star bill and a large following you just might get away with budgeting on 60% capacity, but you have to be very sure of your product and I would advise no higher for your first event.

Ticket prices, like any other product price, are dependent on your overheads. Decide on the minimum that you wish to make from the event. Try to charge under £10, preferably around the £5 or £6 mark (more in London, or if you know that your area is wealthy with a tradition of high ticket prices) or you will be encouraging fraud (see section on Security). If the sums add up then go ahead. If you need more then remember that it is better to sell more tickets than to put the price up too much so try to increase your audience capacity or make sure that the event is attractive to a broad enough base.

If you need less than your target figure to achieve your objectives consider lowering the price or adopt a multiple pricing policy to attract a wider audience. A full house is a great advertisement for future events and the sponsors will be delighted. Remember, their objective is to reach as many people as they can. Keith Diggle, in his *'Guide to Arts Marketing'*, makes the statement 'If you have to choose, more people is more important than more money'.

Wherever possible, charge one price throughout. This is quite acceptable if you are staging an open air, no seats show. Children may go free. You may find that you need to include concessions for OAPs, those with disabilities, children, UB40 card holders or whatever, especially if it seems appropriate for the benefiting charity but this all goes to reduce your income and complicates ticket sales. The advantages are, however, that you may well be reaching an audience that you otherwise would alienate, increasing your sales and developing an audience for future promotions. The choice is yours. If you are to structure your ticket pricing use as few options as possible.

Pricing checklist

❑ Be realistic when working out your budgets.

❑ Keep ticket prices down and sell all the seats.

❑ Keep the pricing structure simple.

Booking your acts and what you get

Your objectives are to book an act or acts that everyone wants to come and see so do your research properly as detailed earlier in this chapter.

Booking your act options

There are a number of ways to book your acts. You can:

1. Use *'Showcall'* or *'The White Book'* (details at the back of the book) to find what you want individually.
2. Use an agent to put the whole event together for you.
3. Work in partnership with a local concert hall or theatre.
4. Use contacts.

Depending on who or what you book as entertainment you will have to supply all, some or no sound and lighting equipment. It is probably true to say that all popular, amplified music acts come with a complete package of lights, sound and a planned stage show with a full operating crew. Many bands include pyrotechnics or lasers in their shows. Some comedians such as Jim Davidson go out with the whole works as if they are operating as a pop concert.

Other one-person shows may supply basic lighting if you are lucky but require you to supply everything else from curtains to pianos.

You can see by the above that finding the right person or band is not the whole story. If you are attempting an outside event for the first time, then I would advise getting the best and most professional help that you can afford. Much better to have to pay the experts and make only a small profit in the first year than have to explain a £10,000 deficit. After a few events you might feel confident enough to organise more elements on your own.

If your event is small and you have some experience and know where to look for technical assistance or are booking a tent with full equipment and crew facilities, then looking for the acts you want in the directories may be enough for you (*Option 1*).

If you are less confident of your research and have no idea of where to go for entertainers or equipment, then the right agent can supply you with as much or as little as you need. She or he can offer just the acts themselves or put together the whole show with all the lighting, sound, fireworks and even the stewards (*Option 2*).

In some areas you may find that a trip to the local theatre might work wonders for the spirit of 'entente cordiale'. Instead of looking on you as some kind of opposition the theatre manager might be prepared to treat your event as an extension of his/her theatre. She or he might be prepared to act as agent for you, she or he would know most of the legal and health and safety requirements and might very well jump at the chance of something a bit different. Of course, unless you are very lucky, it is unlikely that you will be able to employ this paragon for free, so you will have to advertise the theatre (make sure that you will not be staging competing events) and guarantee a donation (*Option 3*).

Finally, you might be lucky enough to be involved in the music world, classical or pop, which is why you have been asked to organise the event. At the risk of working friendships, shamelessly pull strings and beg favours but, as with the sponsors, be aware what you can do in exchange. Offer publicity opportunities like they were going out of fashion. Throw a thank you party for all who helped and offer a reasonable amount of free guest tickets. Write thank you letters to all and inform people what the final figure is. People really do like to know. If the budget runs to it, employ a photographer to take photographs of all the volunteers so that they have a memento of a great occasion. You will be more likely to be greeted positively when you ask another time, if you don't take advantage of people without showing that you are grateful. This has always worked for me! (*Option 4*).

Booking acts checklist

❑ Consider the four options for booking entertainment.

❑ Look at how much equipment comes with each act.

❑ Treat your contacts and volunteers well.

Cancelling a show

Sadly, one of the less glamorous aspects of being an events promoter is when you have to make the hard decision to cancel a show. And it may be for a number of reasons.

Reasons for cancellation

1. Extreme weather conditions.
2. Unavailability of the main act.
3. Inadequate ticket sales.
4. Lack of sponsorship.
5. Opposition.
6. Mounting additional costs.

Reasons 1 and 2 are completely out of your control and if it pours down for 48 hours before the show or your main headliner act contracts food poisoning it is just very bad luck. The show must be cancelled if there is no viable Plan B. It should be stressed, however, that extensions of consequential loss insurance and rainfall cover should be obtained to cover your losses for this kind of eventuality.

Reasons 3, 4 and 5 might be thought to be rather more in your control. Sometimes a reason for an unexplained lack of interest in a show is hard to find, and occasionally the event may have been unlucky enough to clash with something that proved unexpectedly popular. In general, though, you should be able to point the finger at inadequate research, or ill-prepared or non-professional proposals and there is no excuse for lack of preparation. Make sure that your benefiting charity has been honest with you about any unpopular activities it may have been involved in. They may be projecting the wrong public face and it may not be the right time to stage an event of this kind.

Reason 6 is unforgivable. Before you firm up on your ticket prices you must have quotations for all your major outlays. You should be able to produce a reasonably accurate budget for all other expenditures and include a pretty hefty buffer fund (see section on pricing). By the time you actually go to print with your publicity you must know your profit margin. If too many unexpected costs keep creeping into the equation, you may not have to cancel completely if you catch the disease earlier enough. Consider delaying your event until you are really sure of what you are liable for.

It is better to cancel an event too soon rather than too late. You may be able to save at least some of the costs or arrange to hold the event another time.

How do you let people know that it is cancelled? You have three groups who need to know. First, those who may have already bought tickets and parted with their money; second, those who were intending to buy tickets sometime in the future or turn up on the day; and lastly, those who are involved in the event itself.

You need to decide what your policy is with regard to those who already hold tickets. There are a number of options.

What to do if you cancel
1. Return all ticket money.
2. Exchange tickets for a voucher to be used at any future event if you are planning a series or refund the money.
3. Honour the tickets and hold the same event at a later date or, again, refund the money.

The job of refunding money is made much easier if you are

employing a professional ticket sales service, although you may have to pay extra for this service. Be aware that tempers can run high especially if people are very disappointed or have made special arrangements to attend. Again the advice 'the sooner the better' is important.

When you have decided what the appropriate action is you need to advertise the cancellation. The cheapest way to inform the public is to send a Press Release to newspapers and radio stations and offer interviews to explain the decision. Running official advertisements in the press cost extra money and you need to control your losses as far as possible. Remember to cancel all further publicity and paste cancelled stickers over posters advertising an information number, wherever possible.

Those who have yet to buy tickets will benefit from the media reports. Keep any ticket outlets open for a few days, as much to provide information as to refund money. Remember to inform those who may have been attending free of charge or in a VIP capacity.

You will also have the unenviable task of contacting everybody who has anything to do with producing the show – volunteers, suppliers and services. Do not forget anyone. Negotiations may have to start about payment or part payments that may still have to be made. Your job will be made easier if you previously met this eventuality head on when you negotiated a price in the first instance.

Cancelling checklist

❑ Work out a cancellation policy in the planning process and allow for cancellation in the contracts.

❑ Consider delaying or postponing the event if possible.

❑ Cancel as soon as you are sure you must.

❑ Ensure that you let everyone know.

At the end of the show

After a huge event such as has been described you may well feel you are in a state of collapse. Don't leave for your well deserved rest too soon as there will still be work to be done.

Apart from ensuring that the site is clean and tidy and that everything is left in a safe condition until it can be collected, you need to bring your volunteers together for one last time to offer them a big thank you. I cannot stress enough that volunteers are frequently the backbone of charity fundraisers and although they often have a great time, the work is hard and time consuming and they should not be taken for granted. Write thank you letters where appropriate.

You should try to pay your bills and clear your debts as soon as possible, so that you are able to make a cheque presentation to your benefiting charity not too long after the event itself. Remember to organise some press coverage of the presentation itself, and invite the sponsors and anyone else you might think would like to be there.

If you are pleased with the final result and you plan to repeat the whole thing again another time, start thinking about gathering your organising group together no later than two or three months after the last event. Hold a debriefing and learn by your mistakes. As you gain experience you may be able to rely on less and less costly professional help, but don't let go too soon. You only have to run one disastrous event and you will lose a hard won reputation overnight.

And the last word

Try not to panic about the actual day. If you plan properly, employ the right people and go to the professionals for advice, you will find that the day will almost run itself.

End of show checklist

❏ Check the site for safety and cleanliness.

❏ Show your appreciation to your volunteers.

❏ Settle all bills as quickly as possible.

❏ Make a splash with your presentation and extend the press coverage.

❏ Consider repeating the event.

❏ Learn by your mistakes.

❏ Don't abandon professional help too soon.

EVENT 3

Orienteering

EVENT 3
Orienteering

Orienteering is one of the few sports that can be truly said to involve the whole family as long as you are actually mobile – even very small babies can be introduced to orienteering from the dizzy heights of a back pack.

Although it is a sport combining athleticism and intellect, you don't have to be very fit or very skilled to enjoy it at the basic levels, and this makes it perfect for a fundraising activity as it appeals to complete novices and elite orienteers alike. A one day event of a few hours can include courses geared to toddlers and to the top national competitors, and there are age classes from under 10 right up to 70 plus.

There is also a version of Orienteering known as Trail-O especially designed for people with disabilities and learning difficulties with wheelchair-navigable paths.

Money is raised through a combination of sponsorship and entry fees plus a few other fund-swellers as appropriate.

The ethics surrounding orienteering are particularly attractive. *Rule 1:3* in the official rule book is titled 'Fairness' and includes this statement, 'The spirit of fairness and good fellowship shall be the chief consideration in all aspects of the sport, including the interpretation of these rules'. All through the activity you can expect to find honesty, tolerance and lack of pettiness. This attitude is particularly refreshing in a world that is used to seeing sport surrounded by reports of cheating, court cases and media involvement. It seems wholly appropriate to extend these ethics to an event devoted to charity fundraising.

Orienteering started in Sweden at the end of the First World War. The first orienteering event was held in the UK in 1962, but it wasn't until 1967 that the British Orienteering Federation (BOF) was formed. The JK (Jan Kjellstrom Trophy Event) is orienteering's most prestigious event in Britain; held annually, at varying venues, it attracts around 5,000 national and international competitors.

Why orienteering?

Unlike many other sports – such as road racing, fun runs and marathons – orienteering, because it is a young sport, has not become passe in the world of charity events. Competitors do not feel that they are used and 'bled dry' by continually running for sponsorship; indeed many clubs welcome all the help that they can get to introduce new members to the fun of their sport.

The downside is that it is not strictly a spectator sport, and because of the lack of public awareness competitors do not gain quite the kudos that they might in completing something as famous as the London marathon...yet!

Running has proved a good friend to charity fundraisers, the London marathon in particular, and it is tempting to decide to stay with what one knows especially when we can see past successes in raising thousands of pounds for all sorts of organisations plus the attraction for serious runners which helps gain company sponsorship.

The truth today is rather different. The London Marathon and the Great North Run are said to still be apparently healthy but only due to the enormous waiting lists from past years. Fewer and fewer people are interested in long distance running, and in the future when the waiting lists are reduced we may well see that these popular marathons show a large reduction in fun-runners (the ones that really matter when it comes to raising funds) and the race becomes more of a show-case for the professional marathon runners.

From over 200 marathons held around the country in 1986, nearly ten years later there is only a handful left. Pledges are hard to collect, and in hindsight it has become apparent that long-term road runners can suffer health problems and may wear out their knees and other joints before time.

There is also a maze of rules and regulations surrounding road races. The British Athletics Association (BAF) is an organisation that takes itself very seriously and have had to take the popularity of marathons and fun runs on board for safety's sake. (It is not a job for the amateur to organise a race with thousands of competitors.) Totally chaotic races were being held and worse still, unfit, inexperienced, overweight people were killing themselves all in the name of charity. Quite rightly, something had to be done. Consequently BARR (The British Association for Road Races) was set up, the *'Road Race Handbook'* was written and published, and a system of grading races was devised. All very precise; all very formal. Road racing is for the professional, and if you want to set up a road race there are organisations that can help you do it with all the right knowledge and contacts (details at the back of the book).

There is no doubt that with the right organisers and the right runners these races can still be good fundraisers but you need to find something special to use as a marketing tool. The site might be unique, such as a new stretch of unopened motorway, or as in the case of the Mersey Tunnel Race which took advantage of the fact the Tunnel is unlikely to be closed again for another ten years. But don't try to organise it unaided unless you are very experienced and are very sure of all the regulations. Road races do have their advantages but I think orienteering has many more.

What is orienteering?

Very briefly the sport of orienteering consists of finding the quickest route between a series of control points (three dimensional red and white triangular markers) using a marked map with or without the additional use of a compass. The route you take and the speed at which you go between controls is up to you.

Orienteering usually takes place off road and often through beautiful forested countryside but a course can be set up along streets, in school grounds, parkland or around buildings. Competitors are usually timed individually, but start at one minute intervals at a predetermined time, often disappearing in different directions as soon as they leave the starting box. This obviates the need for a dangerous and sometimes confused mass start and all the safety restrictions that go with it. There are events that do have so-called mass starts, but these consist of groups setting off at intervals and do not have the safety implications of hundreds all setting off together down the same route.

There is no specialist equipment needed to compete at a basic level. Competitors should wear sensible outdoor clothing (not shorts unless the event is held in open countryside) and a good pair of walking or running shoes. A whistle is often suggested as a safety precaution in case a competitor gets lost. A red Biro is sometimes needed to mark maps and at more advanced levels a compass is needed.

. . . .

Getting started

You can't really decide if this sport is suitable for your needs unless you have some experience of seeing an event in action. The best way to learn about orienteering is to actually try it out. Don't worry if you are retired, unfit or have small children. For the purposes of this book my family, consisting of two adults and two children aged 2 and 5 years old, joined the local club and found something that we could all do and enjoy with relative ease.

Contact BOF (British Orienteering Federation) – details at the back of the book – for a list of your local clubs; they should be able to let you have a fixtures list.

Serious planning cannot start until you have more than a germ of an idea and once you have decided that orienteering is for you, your first priority is to find a date and a venue. Again you will need your local club to help you with this.

One vital thing to remember is that although you don't have to register an event with BOF, you would be well advised to do so. Registration automatically ensures that the event is covered by BOF insurance releasing you from the often difficult task of finding one-off, reasonably priced public liability cover.

As with all events, particularly sporting events, you will need to allow several months to organise your event if only to have time to publicise the date in the sporting calendar.

If you need to have a map of your chosen area prepared from scratch, that is from the first survey through to the printed map, you will have to set your sights higher and further into the future. Some maps may take over two years to prepare and can cost thousands of pounds. Don't panic! I'll explain more of this later.

Getting started check list

❑ Contact the BOF and your local club.

❑ First priority is a date and a venue.

❑ Advisable to register event with BOF.

❑ Allow at least 6 months or more if you need a new map drawn.

Getting a committee together

Although an orienteering event is not subject to the same rigorous regulations as a major road race attracting the same numbers and you will not face anything like the same hazards, you are still responsible for organising a specialist event which has special safety requirements. Again this is where you will have to put yourself into the hands of the local club experts and take their advice or follow their directions. Orienteering does have its own rules and the BOF Guidelines which are available for a small fee from BOF. Your event can be quite separate from the club events but it is useful to ask the club secretary or course designer – who can be one of the club's planners – to be part of your organising group.

If you are organising a BOF registered event, and even if you are not, you should use officials who have been BOF trained to the level and experience appropriate for your competition.

A large charity event will also need other officials who may or may not be members of your committee or organising team.

Safety is paramount and you will need a **Medical Officer** from St John Ambulance or the Red Cross as they will probably provide your medical team on the day. The medical corps of the Territorial Army are also a possibility. A few years ago these services often came free of charge, or at the very least for a small donation, now most medical cover needs to be paid for and you should obtain quotations before you go ahead.

As in other events it helps enormously if you can persuade a **Representative from the local press** to be involved. He or she can work out a marketing plan for you and ensure that articles are included at the optimum times. Entry forms can be printed in the paper and perhaps they will print a programme and the list of finalists after the event.

Other, less specialist help will also be needed and because of the enormous amount of administration that is involved you may find it necessary to appoint an **Entires and Sponsorship Co-ordinator** and you should not operate any committee without a **Treasurer**. You should be able to get away with the above as a central core committee. Others could have non-executive duties but attend meetings from time to time to report on progress. Perhaps the **Chief Marshal** and **Caterers** should be under this heading. On the whole I feel that a committee should be kept to a minimum. Anything above ten members gets seriously unwieldy, and I have had to sit on committees that have consisted of twenty five or more which is hopeless if you want to get home before midnight! Don't forget to appoint a **Minutes Secretary** too.

Finally, if you are clever enough to attract a major **Sponsor** they may insist

---

Officials you will need

As in other sporting events orienteering has its own team of officials.

Organiser: is in charge of the competition part of the event and may appoint other officials.

Planner: designs the course and is responsible for marking the courses onto the maps and preparing the control description lists. She or he also oversees the correct placing of the control markers prior to the start.

Controller: checks the work of the planner, ensures that the courses are fair and are organised in accordance with BOF rules. The Controller must be qualified and could be described as the top person in the hierarchy.

Mapper: is necessary if an area has not been used for orienteering before. S/he will also be responsible for obtaining any permissions of copyright.

Committee check list

❑ Obtain BOF rules.

❑ Ask local representative to be part of your organising team.

❑ Appoint officials for core committee.

❑ Consider other duties and recruit help accordingly.

❑ Look for major sponsor.

on having a representative as part of the committee. This is often an advantage because they are on the spot to see you working really hard but perhaps struggling to glue one vital piece together due to lack of funds, and it is at this stage that they may be prepared to add a bonus. A company sponsor may be able to supply volunteers to help with the marshalling, setting up and other event duties.

Choosing a date

The date may need to take account of other events in your area and possibly nationwide, especially if you intend to invite some elite competitors for extra publicity. High summer should be avoided if possible; orienteering traditionally takes place between September and May due to the height and density of vegetation in the summer months as well as the occasional hot spell. Although some summer evening events do take place, it is probably better to stick to traditional dates as you are likely to attract a larger field. An advantage of choosing an event away from the summer season is that you will have less competition from other out-of-doors fundraising events that frequently have to take place during times of limited good weather. Orienteering can take place in any conditions, although for the sakes of the very young and very old try to ensure that the temperature will still be reasonably comfortable and the ground unfrozen.

> **Choosing a date check list**
> ❑ Take account of other orienteering events.
> ❑ Avoid high summer and midwinter.

Choosing the right type of event

Orienteering can take place in many forms, some of which may be more suitable for fundraising events than others.

Families that attend local events will be most familiar with the colour coded events which cater for eight levels of ability and length, though not all grades are represented at every event. Grades go from white (1 to 1.5 kilometres, suitable for 6-12 year olds) right through to Brown (7km plus for experienced adults). More advanced competitors will attend Badge Events (where the competitors only run within their own age class and compete to win official badges), Norwegian Events (where you are only given part of the course at a time) and Night Events. All these events are described as 'cross country'.

There is not much of an opportunity for sponsorship at a cross country event but you could double the entry fee (usually about

£2.50 for adults and £1.00 for children). Consider a family fee for a group all attempting the same course with one map. You can charge extra for additional maps. Comic Relief raised money at one event in Yorkshire by selling headbands for the competitors to wear when they took part.

My advice is to think big! Of course there is a limit to how many people one venue can sustain. But if you are going to the expense and effort of having posters printed, schools packs designed and marketing plans compiled, why not encourage several clubs to all run an event for the same charity on the same date? Who knows, you might get the whole region involved. Or the whole country! ...Now that would be something!

Orienteering in this country is arranged in a group structure. Local clubs stage their own events but are part of a regional organisation (12 in all) which are in turn part of BOF. Several regions might be prepared to hold local events all on the same day, charging an increased registration fee, with proceeds all to go to the chosen charity.

The advantage of choosing the above option is that you, the fundraiser, are really only involved in the marketing of the actual idea and the persuasion of the selected regions to assist you. The events themselves are already part of the regional calendar and have a fairly captive audience.

I realise that many people reading this chapter will never have seen a cross country event for real, so I include a small description of what you might expect to see at a local colour coded event. Apologies for those who are familiar with the sport and see many details omitted: it is intended to be a taste only.

What happens at a cross country event?
A typical event is held on a Sunday between 10.00am and 3.00pm or 4.00pm. People arrive (almost always by car) during the first few hours and register at the appropriate tent, table or car. On registration you are given a map and punch card for the level you have chosen, and a start time.

You then make your way to the start point which should be fairly near. The basic levels are given a master map from which to mark their route before they start, but the more advanced may have to mark their maps after the start (to be included within their elapsed time). Most large events provide pre-marked maps, and you may choose to use this system for a fundraising event as it may be hard to provide enough master maps or space for a large field of competitors to mark their own.

The start will probably consist of a box marked out on the

ground, a gantry over the far limit of the box marked *'start'*, a digital 'clock' (manual or otherwise) in front of the box and two or more officials.

On reaching the start you hand in your stub from the punch/ control card marked with your name, registration number of the vehicle in which you arrived, age class and course colour together with your given start time. The clock will alert you to your turn and at the appropriate time your start time will be called and you will be asked to stand in the box. There may be others starting at the same time but they will be attempting a different course. At the whistle you start your run to the first control point using your skill at reading the map and looking at the terrain. For more advanced grades you will need to use a compass to plan your route.

Each control should be reached in the correct order, the number on the control corresponding with the number and description given on the map. At the control several pin punches will be available to punch a pattern unique to each square on your punch card. There will be two or three punches available for use in case several competitors reach the control point at the same time.

When all the controls have been found and marked, you run for the finish which is usually marked by tapes and arranged as one or more funnels under another gantry. Your time will be taken and punch card collected and matched up to the stub to ensure that you have completed the course. Because the starts are set off in succession you do not know who has won until the end of the competition. Most events provide a postal service for competitors who do not want to wait until the final placings have been worked out.

The second type of event is known as a 'Score Event'. It is this latter event that might be the most use as a successful fundraiser. An added advantage is that it involves considerably less organisation as you do not have to work out an actual course. The competitors do this for themselves but it may not appeal to the purist orienteer. On the other hand, if you are canny in choosing your marketing angle you will attract a much broader base of people new to the sport as well as a core group of committed, national status competitors to run as 'buddies' or attend as VIPs.

What happens at a score event?

Registration is largely the same as for a cross country event except that there is no grading system. You may be given a map sealed in a paper bag that you open at the start to ensure that

The golden rule for cross country orienteering is for all competitors to give that all important punch card back to an official even if they do not complete the course. If there is no card to match up with a stub it will be assumed that person is lost and still in the forest somewhere. A search party will be despatched to look for them even if, in reality, they are tucked up in front of the fire eating their tea.

you don't begin to plot your route before the competition. At an event where you expect many first-timers you may choose to only give out sealed maps to experienced competitors.

Controls and pin punches are the same as for all orienteering events and so are the features and symbols shown on the maps, but there the similarity ends. The objective is not to complete the course in as quick a time as possible but to visit as many controls and points as you can, in any order you like within a given time, usually one hour.

Score events are frequently held on open land, particularly if many young or first time competitors are expected. Sometimes you will be able to see most of the controls reasonably clearly.

Many people may have the same start time as yourself. At the start you hand in your stub as before and wait for your call. Groups of twenty or thirty may be started at five, ten or fifteen minute intervals.

Controls are rated by a point system. Those nearest to the

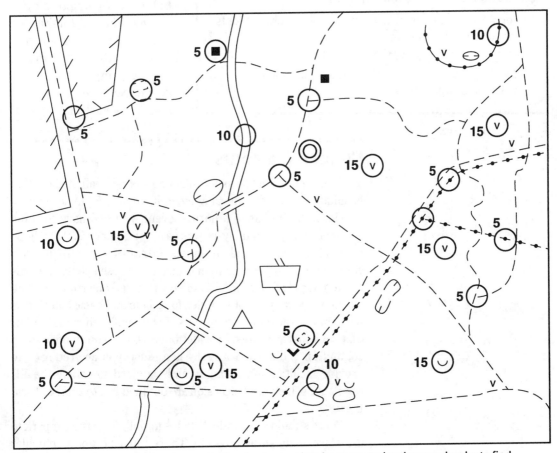

Control markers for a typical score event, showing how points increase as they become harder to find.

start and finish are given fewer points than those more hidden, further away and reached only through difficult terrain. You are responsible for your own timing and points are deducted, or penalty points incurred, for every minute over time.

When you judge that an hour is almost up (from the start time written on the top of your punch card) you run like stink for the finish funnel and hand your punch card in as before. Results may be given on site or the organisers may operate a postal results system.

For a quick, relatively painless result you may choose to go for the cross country option and accept that it has lower fundraising potential. You may be able to repeat the idea several times regionally or go for the 'big one' and suggest a national orienteering fundraising day. I suggest that you work closely with your local club or a regional representative to achieve your objectives.

However, if you feel brave and would like to meet the challenge of organising a relatively untried fundraising event, we can go forth together boldly into the unknown and look at my and more experienced orienteers' ideas for score events.

Choosing the type of event checklist

❑ Consider raising money at existing cross country events and joining up with several clubs (or even the whole UK!) if you don't want to organise a whole event.

❑ Consider a Score Event if you need more funds and welcome a larger challenge.

Choosing a course

Your local club will have specialist knowledge of all the land that is suitable for an orienteering event in your area. In addition to providing the needs of a normal event, you will have to think about providing a suitably large area for parking cars. If you hope to attract a thousand or more entrants you will need a considerably bigger area than is usual for these events, and this is often hard to find around a densely forested environment. You will need extra space or facilities for toilets and basic catering as well as several registration tents. Incidentally, there is no law that says that you must provide toilets, but if you choose to do so, and for a big event it really is a must, you are required to provide facilities of a quantity and standard to satisfy the EC regulations. Details of provision are outlined in *'Organising Local Events'*.

There should be as little distance to walk from the car park to the start or finish as possible. There must be good vehicular access to the car park as competitors may want to come and go continually throughout the whole event, and it is important that pedestrians can be directed right away from the cars as soon as possible for reasons of safety.

The idea of this fundraising event is to provide a course that even quite young children or completely inexperienced people can try with some success. With this in mind it might be sensible to plan your course in parkland, lightly wooded areas or on open heath-land. The grounds of a large country house would be ideal, as the venue will attract visitors in its own right as well as spectators and competitors for the event. Large city parks might well be possible and the grounds of Universities are often popular sites.

Try to avoid a site where the car park is separated from the course by a public road. If this is inevitable, ensure that you can provide a safe crossing point away from junctions or corners and place marshals on the site if necessary.

If at all possible choose a site that has already been used for an orienteering event. The drawing up of new maps is a very expensive outlay as mentioned in the introduction, and your setting up costs will be greatly reduced if you can use existing maps or at least use land that has already been surveyed specifically for orienteering. Many parks, universities and grounds have been used before and BOF carry a register of all the orienteering maps ever made for this country. It is the small matter of a short telephone call to check if your chosen site has been previously surveyed.

If you do choose to use land that has not been traditionally used for the sport you can assure landowners that long term impact is slight even with a very large event. Sensitive areas, bird nesting sites, sanctuaries or cropped spaces are all avoided and 'out-of-bounds' areas are clearly marked in accordance with the landowner's wishes. Although there may be over a thousand competitors all using the course over a period of about 2 hours, because the starts are staggered and runners set off in different directions, competitors are widely dispersed throughout the area very quickly. Many landowners remark on how few competitors there appear to be.

Choosing a course check list

❑ You need a considerably larger support area (for parking cars, etc.) than is usual.

❑ The assembly area should be within easy distance of the start and finish.

❑ Choose a course suitable for all groups with special consideration for the young and first-timers. Consider spectators' needs also.

❑ Try to use an area previously used for orienteering.

❑ Always remember the importance of maintaining the good relationship between landowners and orienteers.

Both the Nature Conservancy Council and the Ramblers' Association have recorded observations on the impact of orienteering events on the environment and comment very favourably. It is important to keep the good reputation that the sport has enjoyed, and it is with this in mind that I stress the necessity of involving existing clubs and groups.

Administration

Having planned your route, the date that the event is to take place and pulled a committee together the hard work of administration has to start. The bulk of this work will fall to the **Entries and Sponsorship Co-ordinator** or **Entries Secretary**.

If this is the first fundraising orienteering event you have organised you will have to advertise for your competitors from scratch. Subsequent events will be easier as you will have a reliable mailing list to work from. You may choose to leave 'recruiting' competitors to the marketing team or it could be the job of the Entries and Sponsorship Co-ordinator. Advertising is laid out in detail under the section on Marketing.

The first task is to open two bank or building society accounts (the treasurer may wish to do this). Free banking is often offered for the first 12 months so check first that your account will be exempt from bank charges. Choose a big company that has many branches. This will be important after the event as many people will want to pay their sponsorship money into their local branch.

What each competitor should be sent

Each competitor must be sent as soon as possible, if not by return post, the following items:

1. Confirmation of entry and notification of receipt of their entry fee.

2. A waterproof number to be pinned on the front (black on white or red on white depending on whether the competitor is entering for 30 mins or 1 hour). A space should be left to write the start time in large print at the top.

3. Instructions as to how the event works and what is expected from each competitor.

4. A local map of the venue showing approach routes, car parks, registration tents, assembly areas, how to get to the start and other facilities (not the course map).

5. A sponsorship form.

6. A leaflet outlining the work of the charity, what the event is raising money for and how much it needs to raise.

7. A prize sheet detailing all the medals and prizes that will be awarded plus a list of the VIPs that will be connected with the competition.

Two accounts are necessary as you need to keep administration costs separate from sponsorship monies.

As soon as the entry forms start to arrive complete with their entry fee (probably around the £3.00 mark) you can start to amass your administration fund.

You may wish to send the punch cards and control descriptions too instead of giving them out at registration. Orienteers like to transfer the descriptions onto their punch cards before the race and an opportunity to fill in the other details on the cards in advance may cut down the crowds all milling about the assembly area.

You need to make a decision about what to do about competitors who come in late. Traditionally, participants are docked penalty points from their overall score but at a fundraising event you may wish to choose a different method as this system will directly reduce the amount of sponsorship money coming in. Alternatively, you could insist that there is no finisher's medal for those who take over the allotted time although the competition is run without using penalty points. Whatever happens you must stress **the importance of handing in the punch card even if they abandon the course.** This system ensures that your sponsorship money is not reduced by incurring penalty points or by the loss of a card, but nevertheless encourages people to finish at the proper time. One orienteer I suggested this to thought it was rather mean to deny competitors a medal. Think about it carefully and be sure to publish this part of the rules particularly carefully.

The instructions sheet should be friendly, un-intimidating, and wherever possible give advice in a positive tone rather than lots of 'Thou shalt not do...!'

Administration check list

❑ Open two accounts.
  1. Administration costs
  2. Sponsorship money

❑ As entry forms and fees come in send out the seven items as detailed above.

❑ Write your instructions sheet carefully and clearly to avoid confusion and any unnecessary questions on the day.

❑ Stress the importance of handing back the punch cards.

Information and instructions

You might consider including the following information after a welcome and thank you message.

1. How a score event works and the objectives of the competition.

2. The start time and when to report at registration.

3. Advice on what to wear.

4. Additional courses (string course, Trail-O etc.)

5. What to do at the finish.

6. State that accurate results by mail are only available to those who finish within the allotted time and who provide a SAE at registration.

7. Confirm that stamped and authenticated sponsorship forms (see below) will be returned with the results. Collecting sponsorship monies is the responsibility of the competitor. Give a deadline by which all money should have been collected and banked in the published account.

8. Suggest where spectators might like to watch from.

How competitor sponsorship works

1. Competitors gather as many pledges as possible during the weeks running up to the event exactly as any other sponsored event.

2. Competitors are divided into two sections. Those who wish to do a 30-minute course (children, families or the elderly), and those who wish to attempt the full hour.

A The 30-minute course is designed so that competitors ignore the point system allocated to each control and just try to visit as many controls as possible within that 30 minutes. Sponsorship is raised accordingly, say 50p for each control.

B Those entering the 1-hour competition build up points according to which control they visit as described earlier. Sponsorship is pledged per point or every 5 points achieved.

3. At the event, no competitor can be registered without first handing in the sponsorship form, complete with signature to show that they have read and agree to abide by the rules of the competition. There should be statement somewhere on the form to the effect that the total recorded after the competition is expected to be paid by the competitor even if they fail to collect all the pledges. Actually, the effort of going through the legal process of suing people for debt is totally impractical, but the thought that they might have to pay the difference is a powerful incentive to collect thoroughly.

At registration (or at the time of posting all the information) each competitor's start time is written in thick black permanent marker on the number which is to be pinned to the clothes. This enables the recorders at the finish to judge quickly whether the course has been completed within the correct time.

4. At the start the stub is handed in.

5. At the finish the punch card is handed over. The stub and card should be matched as soon as possible to ensure that there are no competitors unaccounted for at the end of the competition.

The start time is noted by the recorders and a quick decision is made as to whether the competitor is within the time limit if you are using the rule not to give out medals for those who come in over time.

6. After the event, or during it if you use computers or have a very quick results team, the punch card is matched with the sponsorship form. The total number of controls or points is recorded on the sponsorship form and then stamped to authenticate it.

7. As soon as all the results are compiled the results list and the authenticated sponsorship form is returned to the competitor. A SAE ensures that the results are sent and there can be no prizes without results. This helps to keep postage costs down. To ensure maximum money all sponsorship forms have to be returned come what may even if the SAE was unforthcoming. If the competitor has won a prize a slip needs to be included to say where the prize can be collected or when and where the presentation will take place. There are no cash prizes allowed.

(See Chapter 21 in *'Tried and Tested Ideas for Raising Money Locally'* for more details on sponsorship forms and how to collect pledges.)

Marketing team

Good marketing is vital. You will not have an event at all if you do not get your message across.

Decide on the type of event you are planning to hold. Try to fit the event to the charity if at all possible. For instance if you are raising money for Save the Children make sure that you include a string course for tinies. Advertise your event as a Try-O where families are encouraged to take part. If Mind, or a similar organisation, is your chosen charity include a 'Run-with-a-Buddy' course for competitors with learning difficulties. A Trail-O course for wheelchair users is often popular as is a Relay-O for school children or other teams. All these can run concurrently with the main event over the same course or in a separate area and will be described in more detail below.

Perhaps the venue is the theme. Heritage charities might find a suitable and appropriate course around the grounds of a ruined castle or an environmental charity might consider sand dunes or a heath but be sensitive they may object to the potential erosion.

If you are raising money for a local Millennium project you might choose to invite public figures to take part, or abandon traditional control markers altogether and plot your course using other symbols specific to your community such as heraldic signs. If you are worried that you might trivialise the event, you can keep a traditional flavour for the main course and add a bit of frivolity with the peripheral events. String courses (string is wound around trees or features to show the route to each control) are often marked with favourite cartoon characters or include lolly trees or a treasure hunt. Perhaps you could have 20 historical controls each depicting something from the first century to the twenty-first.

On the whole, I feel that for a large event you should stick to a traditional orienteering system and layout as according to the BOF rules. You will probably receive more help from local clubs who will look on the event as a good opportunity to recruit new interest in the sport. If you ham-up an event too much, some officials might take the view that not only are you exploiting their sport for your own ends but that you are degrading it as well. If you keep things simple and familiar, at least to start with, regular competitors will know what they are getting and are more likely to give their support. The less people that you have to explain the rules to the better. You might be more sure of a positive reaction from local clubs if you gain general approval from BOF first.

As soon as you have decided on a date you should advertise

it in the national calendar, unless your event is very far removed from real orienteering, by contacting the one widely read specialist magazine on the subject. *Compass Sport*, incorporating *The Orienteer* (addresses at the back of the book) is available only on subscription and won't be available to newcomers to the sport from the newsagents shelves, but particularly if you wish to attract national competitors, a date in the fixtures list is a must.

Contact all the local clubs and from them find out the addresses of any specific groups or teams from schools or youth clubs who would like to take part. You can ask your regional Sports Council representative to advise you on possible local interest, and the officer in charge of Sport Development at your local government council offices might be able to suggest more areas. That takes care of people who are already familiar with the sport, but you need to get at those who have never heard of orienteering let alone tried it.

Schools are a very fertile area for sport and this is the one market that it may be acceptable to approach 'en masse'. Orienteering is now part of the school curriculum in Secondary Schools, but it will be new to many Primary Schools. With the help of a local club, make up a good schools pack. You will probably need sponsorship to pay for this. Companies particularly hoping to aim their marketing at children may be worth approaching. Include information about the event, orienteering in general, local permanent courses and clubs. Add a sheet on the charity and how much you are hoping to raise, and what it is for. Include a request form for an orienteering volunteer to meet the head teacher to discuss team entries or talk about a training day. Include a special schools application form to compete in the event. BOF already provide School Information Packs and may be willing to donate leaflets (these used to be sponsored by the TSB) about the sport for your use. You should also explain that it is a family sport and suggest that parents and siblings of school children should be included.

Local newspapers are probably your best way of dissipating information to the general public. Send a press release or ask for an appointment with an interested journalist to explain the project about three months before the event if you have not recruited one on to your committee.

This is the one opportunity that you have for pushing the needs of the charity as opposed to the delights of the event. Make sure that you have photographs available and always fundraise with a specific project in mind. Newspapers are not interested in generalisations. They need facts, the more dramatic the better, some good 'before' pictures so that they can run a final article with the 'after' shots to conclude the story, and a contact who is articulate and knows the charity and the event inside out. Release a target figure and explain how you hope to raise the rest of the money if it is not through this one event. Nearer the time the interest will be all on the event itself and not what it is in aid of.

Find a personality to open the event. Try to persuade some of Orienteering's top competitors to compete in an elite group at the start of the event, or they might be prepared to run with a young person. A competition about orienteering run in the local paper a couple of weeks before the event might offer this as the main prize. The winner and runners up could also win a compass to use on the day.

Don't forget to include the charity's patron. They might prefer to visit or open the event, but you may find that they would be just as keen to take part themselves along with other sporting stars or TV personalities as good PR for both the sport and the cause.

Five or six weeks before the event send another press release explaining the event in detail, and arrange to publish actual entry forms rather than an application address. This will save on printing and postage costs. You may have to pay for entry form inserts, but you should be able to negotiate free advertising or special rates if you offer marketing opportunities to the Newspaper company.

Particularly if this is your first event, you would be well advised to publish a cut off date by which all entries should be received. My experience of being part of a Marathon organising committee showed me that people are very lax about sending in entry forms. Notoriously over 50% come in during the last few days, and it takes an army of people working around the clock to process them. You can help avoid this by offering an early-birds discount. Some events even publish two or three dates each increasing in price as you approach the competition date. You will need to make arrangements for entry on the day but it helps if you can get the bulk out of the way beforehand. At the very least you need to allow yourselves time to get the returns in the post and delivered before the competition date.

> **What information the publicity should include**
>
> 1. Date
> 2. Time
> 3. Venue
> 4. Who the event is suitable for
> 5. What it is in aid of
> 6. Who is organising it, a contact address & an information telephone line number
> 7. The types of event that are included
> 8. How to enter and where to pick up an entry form
> 9. What to bring if entering on the day
> 10. How much it costs

Try to get the entry form printed in the local paper every day for a week. Entry forms for collection, posters, leaflets or other printed publicity need to go out at this time too.

Make sure that all publicity is heavy on the family aspects of the sport, and the fact that it is suitable for first-timers, the very young and the very old. Make the whole event look FUN.

Sports shops and outdoor clothing shops might be prepared to stock entry forms for you, and if your charity has its own shops or offices, entry forms must be available from these outlets also. Remember libraries, community centres, sports halls and even Tourist Information Centres make good pick-up points.

Make sure that people know what prizes they are competing for on the posters as well as on the instruction leaflet.

Two weeks before the event send another press release giving the amount of people that have entered. Stress the uniqueness of the opportunity, the splendour and attraction of the venue, its size, the VIPs and person-alities that will be there. Perhaps the landowner might have a special message about the venue. Remember to send a positive invitation to people who have never heard of orienteering and encourage non-competitors to enjoy the environment, to bring a pic-nic or just to spectate. It is a day to try a new sport as well as making a very important contribution to a good cause. Fire people's enthusiasm.

Because orienteering is such a new sport you might arrange to provide an infor-mation line, especially if the event proves very popular. Your sponsor or charity may dedicate a telephone number for you as long as you arrange to staff it with knowledgeable

Marketing check list

- ❏ Tailor the type of event to the benefiting charity.
- ❏ Large events should stick to traditional orienteering layouts.
- ❏ Advertise in national fixtures list. Use *Compass Sport.*
- ❏ Contact local clubs, groups, teams and schools.
- ❏ Contact regional Sports Council.
- ❏ Contact local council Sport Development Officer.
- ❏ Prepare schools package.
- ❏ Look for sponsors for specific areas.
- ❏ Try to negotiate sponsorship deal with local press to cut your advertising costs. Prepare marketing schedule for press releases.
- ❏ Always fundraise with a specific project in mind. Arm yourselves with facts, photos and a good angle.
- ❏ Book VIPs.
- ❏ Consider run-up competitions.
- ❏ Invite patron and ask how they wish to be involved.
- ❏ Consider publishing cut-off date for entry forms.
- ❏ Emphasize the fun side of an event.
- ❏ Encourage spectators too.
- ❏ Consider running an information line.
- ❏ Build in a date for assessing if the event should be cancelled or proceed.
- ❏ Remember to publish the final figures and send press releases to keep the event fresh a little longer.

volunteers. Alternatively you could tape further information and advertise an answerphone number.

When people return a completed entry form together with the fee you will send them basic instructions on how orienteering works (see section on Administration). For those who enter on the day there is no such opportunity so you must ensure that your publicity includes all the fundamental information about the event.

All of which is quite a lot of information to present well. If space is at a premium then you can leave points 7, 9 and 10 to be answered on the information line.

Above all do not be afraid of cancelling or postponing the whole show and admitting that you may need to wait a while for the time to be right. You should build in a time when this decision must be addressed if necessary.

After the event, when you have counted up all your pledges from the sponsorship forms, you can send out a press release describing the event and stating the amount pledged. Of course, you may not receive all the pledges but you can publish the final figure when you hold a small reception (to which the press are invited, naturally) to stage an official hand-over of the cheque to the benefiting charity.

Don't forget to send a final press release when the project for which you were fundraising is complete. You get another boost for the charity and it just might tie in with the build up to another orienteering event.

. . . .

Company sponsorship

Although the entry fee should cover your expenses any sponsorship money that you can obtain will greatly add to the fundraising potential of your event.

Sponsorship is useful in kind as stated above. Never underestimate the usefulness of the media or its expense if publicity has to be bought. Any advertising or coverage offered free of charge should be accepted with gratitude. Local radio as well as the press is often a good source of sponsorship.

Orienteering competitors do not always need specialist clothing or kit to take part but nevertheless special suits, shoes, arm and leg protectors (bramble bashers), map cases, compasses and other equipment are manufactured. There is even the odd specialist shop or supplier providing nothing else. I doubt that you will negotiate a major sponsorship deal with these companies but it is a good place to go for specific needs – perhaps the registration tents or payment for the maps. You can offer a free pitch to sell their products as well as the company logo on sponsored items.

It is greatly to the advantage of the event and the benefiting charity if you can find a major sponsor. This is not such an easy task and it may be better to wait until you have some feed back as to the numbers of runners that you hope to attract. It is well worth putting together a professional sponsorship proposal as described by Mick Bennett of Sport for Television, in *Tried and Tested Ideas for Raising Money Locally'*. You should, however, not rely on outside backing and if you find that you unable to balance the books without company sponsorship you should look to the viability of the event. All money raised by the competitors should go to the charity; administration costs should come from entry fees. Company sponsorship gives you the wherewithal to spend more on PR, information and advertising as well as offer more to the charity. As stated above, maps can be a very expensive item. However, they are a perfect advertising medium. Think what you can offer the advertiser. Every competitor has to have one. They are all in waterproof bags, and they are frequently kept as a momento of they event. What more could any advertiser ask for?

You have both the front and the back to consider. If you print the map in the middle of the paper leaving a three inch border all the way round you should be able to sell 18 or 20 squares at the very least. Remember not to make the map too big; about 18 inches square is about as much as anyone can handle without it becoming a liability.

On the reverse you have a free rein. You could sell three inch squares all over or a large patch in the middle and smaller ones around. You could run another competition where you charge another small fee to enter or you could use the space for information about the country code. You may find a sponsor for the whole thing or you could use the area for a message or a thank you to each competitor from your charity. (Read *'Sell Space to Make Money'* for more ideas, details at the back of the book.)

The control descriptions offer another opportunity, frequently printed on Tyvek or other waterproof material, they are virtually indestructible, usually have the back

---

Company sponsorship checklist

❏ Try to negotiate one or two major sponsors rather than several small companies.

❏ Wait until you have a comprehensive plan for the event and an idea as to how large it will be before you offer sponsorship proposals.

❏ Do not rely on outside backing to make the event viable.

❏ Consider all sponsorship options.

completely blank and can be sent out in advance which gives the advertiser more exposure.

If you are not successful in finding one or two major sponsors another option is to divide areas up into separate compartments so that sponsors have a choice of being associated with the map (as suggested above), the catering and drinks stations, the registration tents, car park, etc.

Results and prizes

Because most orienteering events have a staggered start it is often not possible to produce accurate results and placings on the day of the event. If you do it could mean that some competitors are hanging about for a very long time whilst all the others finish.

Score events frequently have staggered mass starts and only take an hour or so to complete therefore making the possibility of producing the results within half an hour of the first finishers more realistic.

Results at a large event are only really possible if a computerised scoring system is used. Many orienteers will tell you of events held in the depths of the countryside where all the computers have gone down and no alternative source of power to be found. This is no joke when it happens to you and, unless you are very sure of your power source, you might choose to rely on calculators and pencils and send the results out by post at a later date. You will also need to address the possibility that you may have a complaint or an appeal, and you should have a set of rules available and a 'jury' to deal with any competition problems.

Nevertheless, a charity event should go with a swing, and there is nothing like a good prize presentation ceremony to get a good atmosphere going for the end of the event and to round things off on a happy note. It helps if people leave on an up-beat rather than slink away quietly to their cars and disappear. In any case, your patron or major sponsor will probably like an opportunity to say a few words of thanks. So look at the ideas for prizes below and make a selection to suit your event. Try to get a balance of prizes that can be presented on the day with others, perhaps more important to the real orienteers, to be presented later.

As mentioned before, you should not offer cash prizes. However, your event will be very popular if you ensure that you offer an award to all who reach the finish within the time allowed regardless of whether they have visited all the controls.

Ribboned medals are typically used for awards, but many

orienteering events have very creative and attractive completion prizes. Slate coasters are given at some Scottish events, and, famously, one French event gave all the competitors a beautiful wooden yo-yo! Un-polished wooden pens are inexpensive and appropriate, head bands or other equipment, such as wrist bands or map cases might be possible.

Medals on ribbons can be purchased in bulk reasonably cheaply from any trophy shop to be found in the *Yellow Pages*. Volunteers should be ready and waiting to hand out awards to worthy competitors as soon as they are clear of the finish.

Spot prizes can be awarded, perhaps the 100th person over the finish line, or the youngest competitor to compete over the 30-minute course or for any competitor who manages to visit all the controls within the hour. Prizes for the most sponsorship money raised or even a prize for a lucky number on the programme or a raffle of entry numbers may help to swell funds and certainly adds extra interest. You will need to sell tickets and make the draw at the event to avoid having to obtain a Lotteries Licence.

You can add to the fun of the day by offering other prizes for the quickest times over the additional courses. If you have attracted a major sponsor they may wish to suggest a category and present a special award.

Competitors who have won cups and prizes will need to have these presented to them near to the finish. Arrange to build a rostrum to stand the winners on (some stage risers borrowed from a school will be perfectly adequate) and a VIP to present the prizes. There may still be other runners yet to finish, but you should not let that delay the prize giving ceremony too long after the first runners come through otherwise they and the spectators will get restless and wish they could go home.

Results and prizes checklist

❑ Decide if prizes and results will be given at the event or later by post.

❑ Allow space for your patron to say a few words.

❑ Do not offer cash prizes.

❑ Do offer a medal to all finishers within the allowed time.

❑ Do offer spot prizes.

❑ Look at all options for swelling funds.

After the event

Immediately after everyone has finished the course and the prize ceremony, if you are having one, you need to check that all the competitors are accounted for. If you think someone may be lost then follow procedures as laid out in the section 'Lost Competitors'.

As soon as possible make arrangements to clear the site. You will probably need marshals to help empty the car park and assembly area. Next, clear the course of controls, retrieving all equipment, markers and tags, etc. If a control point looks particularly worn it may be possible to effect some remedial work there and then, otherwise you may need to suggest that a small team return the next day.

All litter should be removed off site unless you have made arrangements to leave sealed bags or a skip until removal at a later date. Toilet facilities should be cleaned, removed or locked until they are collected. Details outlining 'Loos and Litter' are given in *'Organising Local Events'*.

Cash, sponsorship forms and results lists should be carefully collected and taken to a place of safety.

Finally you need to walk the whole area and check that all is tidy. Arrange to meet your team the next day to complete the next stage.

Decide how you are to distribute prizes that you have not awarded at the event and prepare an information note to be included with the placings list.

Calculate and prepare results in accordance with BOF rules and authenticate sponsorship forms. Match forms with the SAE and post to the competitor together with a results list showing where they came in the field. Those competitors who did not return their forms with a SAE are sent their sponsorship forms with their time or number of controls achieved as above but are denied the placings list. As explained above, the competitors then have to collect their pledges and pay it into a branch convenient to them.

Complete BOF requirements such as sending a copy of the map, the results and form ER3. Your local club should be able to help you with this. Final accounts will have to be completed both as a legal requirement of your charity and for BOF; you usually have a period of about three months to complete this.

Finally it is always much appreciated if you send out thank you letters as soon as possible. Remember to thank the landowner, BOF your local orienteering club as well as all your volunteers. Try to agree a generous figure to be donated to the orienteering club who provided you with help and representatives. They will be able to put it to good use in providing transport for a youth team or other projects that all cost money, they will be much more likely to offer help in the future if you show that you can offer something in return for all their hard work and loan of their equipment.

Safety

Orienteering has one of the highest statistics for minor injuries of any sport, although a score event over open countryside should be fairly safe. Sprains and scratches are the most common. Most orienteering competitions will not allow competitors to take part over a forested course if they are wearing shorts because of the possibility of injury infection. Long trousers or some kind of leg protection is important even on an easy cross country course. At the very least there are bound to be nettles or bracken to contend with.

An hour or more in cold wet weather can lead to a competitor suffering from exposure. Cagoules are often advised or insisted upon if rain is expected. You may need to consider the possibility of including this on the instruction form.

You need to allocate an **event medical officer**: it could be the senior member of the first aid team that have agreed to attend the event. There should be an obvious first aid point in the assembly area. It needs to be well staffed and have several treatment stations.

Areas of low branches should be avoided for amateurs, although these should be marked on the map, the inexperienced might just end up with a stick in an eye. Similarly, courses that young children might be expected to try should avoid water and road crossings.

Some competitions insist that whistles are carried. The internationally recognised signal of six short blasts, repeated after a short pause, tells the officials that someone is in trouble. At a large event where there are many first-timers the use of whistles might be too much of a temptation for misuse and, in any case, they shouldn't really be necessary at a score event. Equipment, including whistles, should be pinned to the clothing and not hung around the neck.

It is sensible to advise competitors of safety precautions in the instructions leaflet, and you might like to include a reminder that tetanus injections should be up to date. Make the prompt non-alarmist – you don't want to put people off but, especially in a high risk area, you have a responsibility to mention it.

To ensure that the mass-starts are as safe as possible, and for additional safety as well as providing good spectator fodder, you should consider putting elite or experienced orienteers amongst the first groups. You will need a suitable question on the entry form to establish this information.

As with all events that take place in open countryside you must know where the nearest telephone is, what the local Doctor's telephone number is or bring a mobile, where the nearest Accident Unit is and, for particularly exposed areas, what the local Police/Mountain Rescue telephone number is. All this information should be made available **before** the event to all officials.

The organising group should also have contingency plans in place for when the event is threatened by adverse weather conditions. Snow, hail, heavy rain or fog may mean postponement or even cancellation. You need to know how you will let competitors know of changes and how long you can keep everyone waiting whilst you give the conditions time to improve. Particularly warm weather may mean a drinks station needs to be provided somewhere on the course.

Safety checklist

❑ Minor injuries are very common, medical help must be available.

❑ Decide if leg protection, cagoules or whistles are a prerequisite of entry.

❑ Plan the course to avoid any obviously dangerous areas e.g. low branches, fallen trees or dilapidated buildings.

❑ Equipment should not be hung around the neck.

❑ Remind competitors of the need for up to date tetanus protection.

❑ Position elite competitors first during mass-starts.

❑ Advise on nearest telephone, doctor, etc.

❑ Make contingency plans.

Lost competitors

It shouldn't really be possible for competitors to get seriously lost at a Score Event in open countryside as many of the controls will be visible; they may well be just overdue. However, organisers of a cross country event do need to address this possibility seriously and it is important to decide who will make up the search party before the start of the event. The last thing you need is to decide that you really have to go out looking for someone only to find that everyone else has gone home.

It has already been suggested that a stub system should be used to help check that all competitors are out of the area. No system is infallible and people do forget to report back. Including a space on the stub for a registration number of the car that the competitor arrived in helps in that you can check if the car is still in the car park.

Some competitions insist that the ignition keys are handed in at the start which ensures that people have to report back. This is only really possible for small events.

The *BOF Guidelines* detail thoroughly what to do if you

Lost competitor checklist

❑ Decide who will make up the search party before the event.

❑ Decide if someone is lost or just overdue.

❑ Use a stub system to include car registrations.

❑ Read *BOF Guidelines* carefully.

❑ Make an assessment before sending out search party.

---

suspect that someone is lost or injured. Broadly speaking you need to assess the age and experience of the competitor, the time of day, the weather conditions and the time of year before you send out a search party. If you do need to search, start from the finish and work backwards.

How to raise extra funds from an orienteering event

Apart from company sponsorship, competitor sponsorship and entry fees there are several other excellent ways to fill the coffers.

The obvious idea to raise extra funds is to charge for car parking but I suggest that this is the one area that you should leave gratis. Apart from the logistics of stewarding the area with cars continually coming and going, orienteers are used to free car parking and may not take kindly to this extra fee.

Operate a refreshments tent and invite some specialist suppliers to attend and bring stands to sell equipment and outdoor clothing. A pitch fee of anything between £25–£50 would be quite acceptable. Some events of over a thousand people charge up to £200.

If your event has gone well you might consider organising another for next year as an annual competition. To encourage entrants to apply next year and keep the excitement going, consider a special five year series of awards. Each year the finishers win a medal (as outlined above). The medals are all slightly different in shape and design but are obviously part of a series. At any time the competitors can buy a special martingale – the sort of thing that horse brasses are displayed on – on which to fix their medals. When a competitor has won five medals she or he is then presented with a further plaque to fix on the martingale and complete it.

String courses or Run-with-a-Buddy schemes could be sponsored like the main course but you may feel that it would be easier, and more fun for the participants, if you were to charge a small entry fee. 20p or 30p a time will not hurt anyone's pocket and if children want to beat their own record they can enter several times. If you include lolly trees or offer all children a packet of Smarties for finishing you may need to raise the fee accordingly.

Don't underestimate the use of collection tins either. It may be a moot point as to whether you need a street collection licence. You do not need a licence if collecting on private land to which people have had to buy a ticket to gain access. Strictly speaking the assembly area might need a permit but the start point may not as competitors will have paid to use the course. Each district council may interpret the rules differently so check if you are unsure.

The ubiquitous raffle is always useful too. The prizes could include an annual membership to the local club, the regional group or to BOF itself. A prize of an annual subscription to *Compass Sport* or a good quality compass or other equipment would also be popular. Numbers must be drawn at the event and you should announce on the programme what time the draw is.

If you want to sell programmes you could print a 'lucky number' on each and use these instead of selling raffle tickets. Make sure you look for prize donations fairly early on so that you can publish them on the prize list.

Ensure that you have a merchandising stand and display of the benefiting charity's work in the assembly area offering opportunities to educate, purchase goods, make donations or buy subscriptions.

Raising extra funds check list

❑ Consider all the pros and cons before charging for car parking.

❑ Offer refreshments for sale.

❑ Invite stall holders.

❑ Operate an awards series to keep interest flowing.

❑ Sponsor peripheral courses or charge an entry fee on the spot.

❑ Use collection tins but check if you need a licence.

❑ Run a raffle.

❑ Exploit opportunities for getting your message across.

Marshals and stewards

You will need a certain number of volunteer marshals or stewards to look after your event besides the course officials. For a large event or one that is held over a large area, it would be sensible to have them in radio contact with each other or at the least with the medical team.

How many you employ is entirely dependent on the type of event, the venue and how many people the event attracts, your local club representative will be able to advise you. You will need at least two at a time to look after the car park and the entrance. There need to be enough to staff the registration tents to prevent long queues forming. You may need helpers to direct competitors

---

Marshals and stewards checklist

❑ Consider supplying some officials with radios.

❑ Clearly define duties and allow enough volunteers to cover for all contingencies.

❑ Provide conspicuous identification.

---

to the start and spectators to the watching areas. If you are selling pitches for merchandise or catering you will need someone to control this area. You may need someone to supervise a crossing point over a road, and there need to be enough helpers and officials to operate the start and finish areas efficiently although your local club should be able to help here.

Don't forget to allow for extra volunteers to operate the collection and cope with the extra work precipitated by the fundraising aspect of the event. Make sure that you allow for change over teams for those jobs that are particularly demanding.

All officials and volunteers should wear conspicuous vests or clothing to ensure that they are easily identifiable. Arm bands are probably not obvious enough for a large event.

Final word

Finally, unless you are a fully experienced orienteer, remember that this event is totally dependant on the co-operation of the British Orienteering Federation and/or a local club. Obviously hundreds of small fundraising orienteering events springing up all over the country might cause them some problems but a few well organised big-timers can certainly help spread the word about the sport as well as the charity for which it benefits. It is to your advantage as well as to theirs to ensure that you clear your event with the relevant organisations before you go too far down the line.

Remember what has happened to sponsored running events and the understandable reactions from some of the professionals who feel that their sport has been hijacked in the name of charity. Go steady, feel your way, take advice and I hope you enjoy orienteering as much as we do.

The Experience

EVENT 4
The Experience

In this chapter we will look at some of the difficulties of raising money in small rural communities. I will outline a very successful fundraising event that is flexible, needs no specialist knowledge or help and can be made specific to individual needs whether it is for a fishing village in the West Country or a small farming community in the Yorkshire Dales. Coincidentally, having spent some time looking further afield for good rural money-making ideas, I stumbled across this idea almost on my own back yard in a little village called Bergh Apton in South Norfolk. You will not raise tens of thousands in one go but you can expect to see £3,000–£5,000 a time for your efforts, especially if you run something along similar lines but slightly different as an annual event and aim bigger and better each time. It was pointed out to me 'that once a village becomes adventurous, it becomes much easier to organise events'.

Many fundraising events are the product of a small number of people who work extremely hard to produce something that other people attend or donate money to. If one is asked to help in some way, it is often easier to contribute money rather than time or experience. Giving money is a conscience salve and then you can forget the other person's problem. Cynical though that statement is, it is often the most effective way to raise money for a remote cause such as aid for a war half way round the world or raising money for research of some rare disease. If we need to raise money for something nearer home, there are other, more interesting, options open to us and it can be beneficial to involve as many people as you can.

Towns and cities have a large pool of contributors to draw from. Street Processions, such as described in detail elsewhere in this book, are a splendid community fundraiser, as are events held in city parks or gardens. But how do you raise thousands of pounds in a rural area for something as important as a village hall? No community centres or sports complexes here to nip down to when the mood fancies; a population of under a thousand will hardly warrant that.

Raising money in a small, rural community needs a very different approach to those described in the other chapters in this book. There is an obvious disadvantage in the lack of people and facilities but there are tremendous advantages too if you look for them. Most of the community are known to each other, if not personally then at least by reputation. Communities are often more static than in a town and will probably consist of families or people who have family near by and feel community minded. Open spaces are often available in the form of greens, commons, large gardens or fields. Occasional unused large buildings such as disused churches or barns may be obtainable. Larger villages may have a recreation area and sports field. Lack of traffic to accommodate is another advantage as are the disparate activities and skills taking place on site and many more unique to each community.

The success of 'The Experience' hinges on the fact that it appeals as much to those who are part of it as to those who are visiting for the day. It is an all too rare opportunity to see into people's lives. The private veil lifts just for a moment to offer a glimpse of what goes on behind closed doors. Of course it is a carefully prepared glimpse, but nevertheless it satisfies the nosey side of us all. Not the malicious, gossipy type of nosey, but a gentle curiosity that wants to see if other folk live their lives like us. There is nothing so interesting as people. Sure the excuse of seeing a lovely garden or a ditch digger in action is a good one, but it is the people that visitors come to see and talk to and that is the heart of a good rural event.

What is 'The Experience'?

'The Experience' is a series of events or activities that take place over two or three days in a village or community that allow people of the surrounding neighbourhood, or further afield, to enjoy what that particular community has to offer.

Many villages have festivals that achieve a similar objective or keep a special day for celebrating something in particular. What is different about 'The Experience' is that it is arranged around a trail, rather than just leaving the visitor to come across an open garden or having to ask where the refreshments are.

Visitors have to buy a map at any place displaying the 'Experience' symbol – Bergh Apton uses a giant sunflower to great effect. The map couples as a ticket to visit all the other places. On the reverse of the map (which shows all attractions marked with a number, car parks, and a scale) is a description of each attraction, when it is open and the facilities that it offers: toilets, teas, things for sale, children's area, etc.

Visitors can choose to do the whole trail or park at a central place and just visit the places that interest them most. If they like what they see but didn't allow enough time they might come back the next day to complete the trail and buy another map.

. . . .

Getting started

This is not an event that needs a large committee to organise it, just two creative and visionary people may be all that is needed but four or five heads together all helps cut the administration work down and gives a good pool of ideas.

The biggest headache for any event of this kind is to raise some money as a kind of pump-priming fund. You can't hire equipment without putting down a deposit first and you need funds to buy tea and biscuits to sell at a profit. If your outlays are very minimal, it may be possible to allow contributors to pay for supplies from their own pockets and reimburse them afterwards. However, if you feel that you can't ask your helpers to chip-in in this way, you might need to hold a jumble sale or a bring and buy sale to get things started. In Bergh Apton the organiser of the flower festival opened his garden and served teas in advance of the main event to raise money for anyone who needed the money to get started.

If you know that your event is to be an annual event to raise funds for continuing maintenance work on public buildings you might consider starting a Friends Group, where people join by annual subscription and receive first refusal for special events, special seats or just an occasional newsletter to bring them up to date with local news. It is a good way to amass a quantity of money in advance but you must make sure that you understand the legal implications of charitable activities.

Much of the thinking work is done for you. You know the type of event – it's whatever the community come up with. You know the venue, well within reason. You might need to decide where the boundaries of the event are. You know who you are aiming the event at – everybody in the neighbourhood and local tourists. The big decision is when to hold it.

Getting started checklist

❑ You need an organising team of two to six people.

❑ Decide if a start-up fund will be necessary and if so, how.

❑ Consider starting a Friends Group.

❑ Utilise what is available locally.

The date

The date is all important. Most events in this country are only really successful during the warmer months. It is perhaps best to avoid the schools' summer holidays unless you are in an attractive tourist area. By the same token, half terms are death to most events. June, July and September are probably the best months to consider. Think about the major activity in your area and work around the busiest times. It is probably unwise to stage an event in the middle of harvest-time for instance.

Remember to check with the local Tourist Information Centre that you are not going to clash with anything major. An Air-Sea Rescue Day a couple of miles along the coast is not going to do your events any favours, nor will the annual Sheep Dog Trials in the next village.

A Friday, Saturday and Sunday are really the only days of the week that you can be sure of a good turn-out. But don't forget that even if you choose September and the nights are closing in, there is much that can be done to take advantage of the earlier dusk. There is more to just eight hours in the day.

Date checklist

❑ Consider the probable weather conditions.

❑ Avoid summer holiday time unless you are in a tourist area.

❑ Check with the local Tourist Board that you will not clash with something major.

❑ Avoid traditionally busy times such as harvest.

❑ Weekends are probably safest.

First stage

Allow nine to twelve months to pull the whole event together. It is better to have too much time and be relaxed rather than trying to push people into doing things more quickly than they really want.

If you have plumped for a summer event try to at least have the first stage completed by Christmas or before. Those people who plan to open their gardens or have plants for sale need to be able to make long term preparations.

Having decided on a date, or at least a possible date you need to inform the rest of the community. Bergh Apton kept the rest of the village informed through a special newsletter that was sent out fairly regularly. You could send a press release to your local newspaper and/or parish magazine to state your intentions and if you are certain of your date advertise this too for people to mark their diaries well in advance.

By this stage you should have got a fairly good idea via the bush telegraph if your idea has general support. If you sense that 'The Experience' is being greeted with suspicion, you may need to do a bit of ground work first by holding a meeting in someone's house to discuss your ideas in more detail.

All being well, the scheme will be met with cautious approval but if you realise that people are not willing to co-operate you should possibly go no further, although you will probably only get a true 'feel' for how the event is being received if you actually visit people. This event will not work unless the majority of the community are behind you.

Assuming that you have a positive response to your 'feelers', now's the time to circulate a 'Round-Robin' letter to everyone and every business in the area which you want to include in the event. Try to address the letter personally if you can. The local Post Office may be able to lend you a Post Code Directory to help you. You may need to recruit a scout group or other volunteers to deliver the letters by hand, if your community is very small, you may be able to deliver them all yourself giving you the added advantage of being able to describe the event in person. Mailing the letters is probably a waste of money unless you have a very remote community.

Write a brief resume of your idea and how you see the trail working. Arrange an 'open-house' meeting to be held in someone's house, and invite all those who may be interested in offering a suggestion. In larger communities you could include an application form with your resume to be returned within a few weeks. The form should have space for the name and address, the type of activity or facility that they can provide (even if it is just a promise of help on the day – not everyone is happy with the idea of the general public having access to their property) and a more general area for people to write in their own ideas. It might be helpful to add a contact name and telephone number so that people can discuss what they have to offer before committing themselves.

If you are fairly sure that you will need people to serve teas, provide cakes, direct cars, sell maps or other duties, you can include a list of jobs requesting that people put a tick beside those where they might feel able to help at no obligation, of course. On the other hand you might feel that it would be better to see what people come up with first. If you leave things open, it encourages creativity. You can always send a duty list round to those who gave an offer of help nearer the time, but the personal approach is probably more likely to give results.

Post a general request for suggestions and help, in the local shops, Post Office, village hall and Parish Magazine just to catch anyone who might not have had a letter. It also encourages people to talk to each other about the idea and gives you a chance to judge the temperature.

If the community is used to doing special annual events such as a flower festival, a drama production or a concert perhaps you could visit the organisers and assess if they would be willing to allow their event be part of 'The Experience'. The more events of this kind that you can tie into the weekend the better your trail will look, the more visitors you will attract and the more money you will make. Of course you will have to allow other organisations to raise money for themselves, or else they will not be happy for their activities to be part of the whole. But you should be able to claim ten percent of profits or sell extra maps and merchandise.

First stage checklist

❑ Allow up to a year to put the event together.

❑ Consider using a dedicated newsletter or use the available press to inform people.

❑ Make sure that you have support before you proceed.

❑ Arrange an 'open house' or a tear-off slip on the resume for people to put their suggestions and help forward.

❑ Use public buildings to advertise for help.

❑ Use local talent.

Second stage

Sort your responses out into three categories:
1. Specific places to visit or activities that people can take part in.
2. General offers of help.
3. Offers of gardens, fields or other venues where something unspecified can happen.

It may be that you realise that you have made a mistake with the date. Perhaps it was forgotten that something happens at that time of year and that many people cannot take part. Don't worry, that is the whole point of starting early. You can always advertise a change of date and ask for more responses.

Send a newsletter or write personally thanking all those in Category 1 for their generous suggestions, confirming the date and indicating that someone will come to visit to talk about their idea or activity in more detail.

Again through the newsletter or by post, you can thank all those in Categories 2 and 3, for their generous offers. Suggest another date for an 'open house' when people can meet again to suggest how they can help. Meanwhile give them the opportunity to keep in contact and make further suggestions if they would like to.

Decide if you need 'bought in' activities such as some fair ground rides or a bouncy castle. You may need to book them now even if you are not one hundred percent certain where you will use them.

Second stage checklist

❏ Sort your responses.

❏ Check that your chosen date is acceptable.

❏ Keep using the newsletter or inform people personally of developments.

❏ Arrange another open meeting.

❏ Book any 'bought-in' entertainment.

Third stage

Gather a meeting of the organising group and look carefully at the Category 1 offers.

Plot them all on a map and see how they lie according to your planned area. It may be that they are all up one end of the village, especially if a good many businesses have responded. You will have to arrange a car park in this area if at all possible.

Ideally you should aim for a reasonable number of interesting places to visit dotted along roads or streets at not too infrequent intervals. Look at the offers in Category 3, and see if you can include venues that will help even the activities out a little and make the event feel tight and bustling. You can decide what to hold on these sites at a later date. If the area does not lend itself to this layout, due perhaps to a very ribbon style of development or a coast road or a steep hill slap bang in the middle of the neighbourhood, then you could treat it as a positive opportunity and introduce tractor rides or a horse and cart to transport people from one area of activity to another. A small extra charge can be made for this.

A main road going through the area should be avoided at all costs because of the obvious danger of traffic. If the village is approached by very narrow, bendy lanes or is at the end of a road, perhaps on a lake edge or beside the sea you may have to ask for advice from the traffic police as to the best way to deal with visiting cars. Invite an Officer to attend one of your meetings and you can discuss the problems fairly early on. It may be that you need to make arrangements to park cars outside the village and visitors walk the trail on foot or go by special transport.

It is important to point out to people gently that they are responsible for finding the activities that they offer if at all possible, paid for from the central budget, of course. For instance a children's play area may need equipment borrowed and transported from other gardens. Volunteers to supervise young children need to be recruited and an inflatable castle may need to be hired. Your position should be co-ordinator of activities and facilities offered by the village; not General Dogs-Body or Sergeant Major. You may have to delegate jobs or put helpers in touch with each other but you shouldn't have to actually pull each area together yourself.

Once people have decided how they are to contribute you may like to visit, possibly at their request, and advise on how best they can present their venue if they are having problems. You will certainly have to be aware how things are developing. It may also be necessary to intervene if you think too many people in one area are attempting the same sort of activity, although this is unlikely.

Third stage checklist

❑ Plot all the offers of activities on a map and decide how it will work.

❑ Arrange car parking.

❑ Supply public transport if necessary.

❑ Ask the advice of the police regarding traffic.

❑ Offer lots of personal advice but make it clear that each person is responsible for organising their own activities.

Places to visit

Many people will feel that what they have to offer may be too modest to interest the hordes of people that you hope will visit your community. I can assure you that sheer curiosity aside there are enthusiasts from all walks of life, and until you try it you will never know who might come out of the woodwork for the chance to talk about Jacob's Sheep, tuning chain saws or the mysteries of hydrangeas with someone knowledgeable, until you try it.

Others might genuinely feel that their gardens or yards are just too small to cope with more than two or three people at a time. If a garden is specially colourful or interesting perhaps it could be viewed from the road only, or if someone has arranged a display of photographs in their front room then you can arrange to give the instruction, *'No more than four at a time'* on the map.

Most villages have at least one large Manor House or Hall, and it is this that will unquestionably be the big draw. If use of the garden has been offered, make sure that you use it well. If the owner doesn't want stalls or steam displays on the lawns, perhaps you might suggest it as a particularly grand place for picnics and it could offer the obvious place for a car park. Bergh Apton is blessed with several beautiful big houses and it is interesting to contrast and compare what the owners have done to them over the years. A photocopied sheet of a potted history of the building and/or family is worth another 20p and all goes to help swell funds.

Some stops on the trail are just purely for looking at and talking to the owners about what is in front of you. But many other places can offer a rolling programme of events. In a way you could look on the whole village as a gigantic fete and you can certainly use many fete ideas as well as the more obvious

---

Attractions and activities

To inspire you here is a selection of attractions and activities offered in Bergh Apton in 1994.

- General builder offering to talk over special problems.
- A light engineering company specialising in tuning racing motorcycles and sidecars.
- Nursery and garden centre
- Private house, with over 3 acres of rare and uncommon plants set in an old orchard.
- Arabian stud: stallions, mares with foals, and a photo display of 40 years of history.
- Private house: bobbin lace maker at work.
- Manor house: award winning Georgian walled gardens and herbaceous borders.
- The Butcher, The Baker, The Candlestick Maker – a fair beside the Village Hall: arts and crafts.
- The Village Hall: refreshments and displays of village history.
- Dried flower growers and suppliers.
- Village shop and Post Office.
- Teddy Bear's Picnic and Play Area: programme of events throughout the day.
- Woodworkers and farm equipment demonstrations.
- Cottage garden and vegetable garden.
- Farm Shop selling produce, bee keeping display and vintage tractor collection.
- Concrete products.
- Deer farm.
- Church with a full programme throughout the days and evenings.
- Hall: Exhibition of art and crafts; bird of prey display; bee-keeping display; water garden.
- Private garden to be viewed from the road.
- Cottage garden, and garden furniture makers.
- Skip company to discuss every need.

A truly eclectic and unique collection! But not, I would suggest, unique in its diversity. Nearly every village can come up with skills, experience and knowledge as interesting as this list. It's the grouping together that makes the event so fascinating.

---

cream teas, cake stalls, barbecues, sales of plants and raffles. (See *Tried and Tested Ideas for Raising Money Locally'*.)

There are hundreds of other ideas that will be peculiar or particularly appropriate to your own area. Heacham in North Norfolk has created a whole 'voyeur' industry around the harvesting and use of lavender. Every day, scores of people pay to travel in a tractor trailer to some remote field and watch a small specialist harvesting machine cutting lavender heads. Provide a charming and knowledgeable guide, and you will have queues of people waiting for such an opportunity – be it fishing for bass off the harbour wall, admiring a sheep dog being put through its paces, watching a potter go through the process of producing a jug, or seeing a mechanised potato sorter at work.

Some areas are fortunate in that they are criss-crossed with green lanes and public footpaths. If your village has a good circular walk, you might like to consider mapping it out in detail and offering it for sale on the day as an additional attraction.

On-going activities

Some ideas for on-going activities, for which you would make an appropriate extra charge, might include:

- Pony rides for children.
- Church activities: flower Festival, musical or sung concert, bell ringing, display of church fabrics.
- Knife and blade sharpening service.
- Best dressed Teddy competitions (different age groups, old Teddies, giant Teddies, grannies' Teddies, etc.).
- Children's play time: a maze from straw bales; supervised trampoline and bouncy castle; assault course for older children. Charge to include ice cream, sausage, crisps, juice, etc.
- Boat trips.
- Guided walk or nature trail.
- Guided tour around historical building or church, etc.
- Building open to the public (e.g. lifeboat station or ancient barn or disused croft, etc.).
- Clay pigeon shoot.
- Table top games evening (e.g. whist drive or chequers or chess or Mr Potato or Beetle or Battleships, etc.).
- Pond dipping for toddlers and their parents.
- Hoe down or disco.
- Pubs could apply for an extended licence and arrange a pub games evening.

A village church is often a good centre to base the event around. In September you could use a Harvest Festival theme. In June you could go back to the more pagan routes of the church and consider the Summer Solstice. Perhaps ideas based around a Christian Church are not wholly appropriate in your area, even in the countryside. We have a large Buddhist community in our community which often comes as surprise to visitors. You might welcome the opportunity to include themes from your own or other cultures to inform and entertain others from a more traditionally English background. Whatever you do, try to include everyone and make it very clear that no one is too young, too old, too humble or too ordinary to contribute. The response system as outlined above will help to avoid alienating anybody.

A fairground set up for two or three evenings on a large field or green could keep the crowds in the area for longer and provides a magical atmosphere to late summer nights. You can either make money by charging the fairground a pitch fee or you can hire the rides and charge customers yourself. (See Chapter 16 in *'Organising Local Events'* for the legal requirements.)

Fourth stage

Work out what you will need for your infills and firm up on where you intend to site the 'bought in' entertainment if you are using it.

When you are clear who is to be involved and what is going where and when you can compile a programme and concentrate on getting your marketing right. Make sure that leaflets are no more than a sheet of A4 and preferably printed on one side of the paper only.

Rather than leave the programmes in piles in local shops to become untidy bundles of paper slipping onto the floor, you might like to provide your own leaflet rack. A stout piece of A3 coloured card stapled onto the wall or door turned up two thirds from the bottom to make a secure folder or pocket, from which the programmes can be taken, works very well. Draw the trail symbol on the outside of the pocket with the title and soon everyone will associate the symbol with the event.

Information to include in the programme

The programme must include:

- The title of the event.
- The days, dates and times.
- The name of the village or community.
- Where to buy a map (anywhere that displays a trail symbol) and what it costs.
- A contact name and telephone number to ring for more details.

You might like to add:

- Special activities, what time they are taking place and the cost.
- Places to park.
- A resume of attractions and who they might appeal to.

Provide inserts in the Parish magazine or local paper if it is not too pricey. If this is not an option open to you, some milk rounds offer a leaflet drop service especially if they operate as part of a franchise company. Aim to cover all the villages within a five mile radius, more if your area is sparsely populated.

Arrange to put a poster up (photocopies on coloured paper will do) or even a programme, if it is not too cluttered with information, in local shops, post offices, village halls, pubs and businesses.

Signs on main roads near the village might help drum up passing trade, but they have to be sited on private land or be up for less than 24 hours if you are not to incur planning permission regulations. On the whole most of your visitors will be very local and, if your cause has a sympathetic ear and is obviously for the good of the community, those local people will often be very generous. Advertising wider afield may not be worth the extra cost and effort.

Fourth stage checklist

❑ Complete your map and programme.

❑ Work out a simple marketing schedule.

❑ Make and supply leaflet 'racks.'

❑ Use a theme or symbol.

❑ Keep your advertising local.

On the day

Having been very busy for the months approaching The Experience, the day itself may well be quiet for you the organisers unless you are supplying one of the attractions. Do spend time to visit as many venues as possible so that you can genuinely comment on people's efforts. Pass the word around during the day indicating how programme sales are going. Apart from encouraging people through a quiet patch it can be useful to know if an influx is expected in the next half an hour where teas are being served or that a mini bus of children is making its way towards the 'Kiddies Corner'.

Arrange for a safe place to be made available to deposit cash or provide a couple of pick-ups in the day, so that each venue is not responsible for hundreds of pounds for long periods of time. Perhaps someone may have a safe to keep the cash in overnight before you can take it to the bank. Remember loose money is a temptation to the opportunist thief, and you would not wish for any of the volunteers to be put in danger through their generosity.

Make sure that everyone knows when they are expected to wind their activities up. Some people may wish to keep the gates open for longer if they see people still wandering about but they should not feel obliged beyond a certain time.

Check that all car parks and public areas have been left scrupulously clean, or at least arrange for a clean up team to visit in the morning.

Afterwards

In Bergh Apton the organisers held a get-together later that evening in one of the houses that had held the Art and Craft Exhibition. This gave them all a chance to have a private look at the exhibition and enjoy the garden without the hoards of the day around. They shared a glass of wine and some nibbles and told horror stories of the event!

I recommend that you do something similar if you can. It extends the feelings of camaraderie that build up over the months, gives an opportunity to thank everyone and helps dispel any feelings of inadequacy that some may experience if something did not go quite the way that they intended.

Publish a last newsletter to let everyone know how much was raised and giving formal thanks to everyone who took part. Choose some new organisers to give the first ones a rest...then get on with organising The Next Experience!

On the day checklist

❏ Visit as many venues as possible.

❏ Keep a running total as to how many programmes have been sold.

❏ Decide how you will keep the money safely. Arrange for overnight deposit in a safe.

❏ Give volunteers a finish time (and publish it in the programmes too).

❏ Check that everything is cleared away at the end.

Sponsored Bike Ride

EVENT 5
Sponsored Bike Ride

F undraising for a school is different from many charity events in that there is a ready-made audience, advertising is easy, the venue is readily available, and you can choose a date to suit your own convenience.

However (isn't there just always an 'however'!), once you have sent every child home with a letter and plastered every classroom and canteen with posters there is little else you can do. You reach cut off point. You are unlikely to attract more than a handful of local people who have no connections with the school. Which is OK if the school is a city based secondary school boasting over a thousand pupils with a corresponding number of event-going parents or guardians, but not so good if the school that desperately needs new computers has less than 50 children and is in a tiny country village. So, how to spread the event wider? And how to fundraise from those who may not be directly interested in the fortunes of the local school?

The obvious answer to me, when members from local PTAs ask me how they can raise more money than the inevitable fete can offer, is to join forces with other schools and pool resources and ideas. But this, curiously, they are most reluctant to do. The problem of which school to use was apparently insurmountable. How to divide the money seemed to cause irrational headaches. And what seemed like plain rivalry coursed through every vein.

I worried the notion like a dog with a bone for about six months, and eventually came up with the following idea which I hope will fit the bill. It is an adaptation from an nearly nationwide sponsored bicycle ride which started in neighbouring Suffolk just over ten years ago and has gone on to grow and develop every year since. I owe a great deal to the Norfolk Churches Trust Ltd who have willingly parted with information, advised me, and at whose event I have acted as an official over the last three years checking off cyclists as they arrived and departed from a nearby beautiful, but sadly redundant Norman church.

What has struck me about this event is the way participants are completely in control of their own pace. There is no pressure to achieve more than they want to, and it is equally suited to those who want a short family bike ride or young, fit people who really like a challenge.

The beauty of an amalgamated schools event is that you can raise money through sponsorship from people who would never have had anything to do with the school at all. You can also raise funds for a separate charity as well as for each individual school, thus spreading your appeal, and further on in the chapter I will explain how.

There are well over 26,500 schools in England – 450 in my area alone. Not, perhaps, equal to the enormous numbers of churches and chapels but, nevertheless, a sizable figure which gives tremendous scope for an event of this kind.

Before tackling any school fundraising project you would do well to read an excellent book called *'School Fundraising – what you need to know'* – details at the back of the book. This book is a guide to law and good practice for those concerned about schools and charitable status, schools and trusts, maintained schools, raising money for schools through PTA events, and so on. It provides a clear beam of light through the miasma of government regulations that surrounds schools that have opted out, those that have opted in and those that aren't quite sure what they are doing but know they cannot operate unless they have some more funds from somewhere.

How does the Bike Ride work?

Cyclists (and walkers, if you wish to broaden the field) are invited to obtain sponsorship to visit as many schools in one area as they can between the hours of 10.00am and 6.00pm on an agreed day. Each cyclist nominates a particular school to benefit from their ride.

Sponsorship money is collected and returned to the regional headquarters.

When all the sums are calculated a distribution of the monies is then made to all the schools. As in the Churches Cycle Ride, you may choose to retain half the pledges to benefit a chosen charity as well as each individual school.

A simple idea that works a treat for the Norfolk Churches Trust but not without considerable pre-planning – what makes this event work is the enormous number of volunteers that have to be recruited. This is a nightmare situation unless you do what the overall co-ordinators of the Church Cycle Ride (the Historic Churches Preservation Trust) do so well, and that is delegation.

How to get started

In this chapter I will explain how to organise a sponsored cycle ride for one area. If you want to include a larger region or keep the whole idea small – at least for the first year or so – then all you have to do is adjust the ingredients accordingly, rather like making a cake. The instructions are the same, it is just the amounts that are different; introduce another layer or two of delegation if that helps.

All education authorities keep a directory of schools which is made available to the public for a charge; £12–£13 is an average price. Larger authorities tend to be divided into regions: Central, North, South, etc. A directory for these smaller areas might cost you about £3.00. The directories give the postal address of each school, the telephone number, and the name of the Head Teacher.

By using this directory you can establish the number of schools in the surrounding area, how far they are from each other and how wide you wish to spread your event.

When you have made a list of schools that might want to participate, you can write a letter of introduction to each Head Teacher. You will need to explain, briefly, how the idea works and that each participating school has the chance to benefit. Include a small form to be returned indicating if the school wishes to join your event and who is to be the contact name at the school; a return date can help move the letter up the pending tray. Head Teachers may feel that they cannot spare a member of staff to take on the event so don't be surprised if most of your contacts are members of the PTA or even senior pupils in schools for older children.

When most of the forms have been returned you should think about forming an organising group if you haven't already done so. If nothing else you will need a Treasurer and possibly someone who can act as typist unless you have plenty of time on your hands. An event involving several elements and dozens of schools is time consuming to get off the ground. Don't forget that you will need a cash float to pay for postage, stationary and possibly telephone calls. You may have to borrow from the parents' group funds unless you are prepared to foot the bill yourself until you can be repaid.

You may have a good idea as to who you could ask to be

Getting started checklist

❏ Obtain a schools' directory from your local authority.

❏ Write introductory letters to the Head Teachers.

❏ Form an organising group.

❏ Decide where your start-up fund will come from.

---

part of the organising team, but if you need extra people you might wish to include an additional question on the form mentioned above asking for people who might be prepared to be involved in a greater capacity.

Choosing a date

Naturally you will need to choose a date during the school term which boils the options down a little. The weather in the Winter and Spring terms is probably too chilly – unless you choose a date in September, but this is the traditional date for the Church Cycle Ride, and it would be to both your advantages not to be too close to each other. Exam-time is bad timing so realistically you are possibly looking at April or May.

A Saturday or a Sunday is a must although you will always clash with somebody's special sports event but check that it isn't the same date as a major inter-schools competition or you may wonder why no one wants to help or take part.

10.00am–6.00pm has worked well for the Churches and is probably as good a time to choose as any. If you find after the first year that there were still intrepid cyclists trying to clock up just one more score at 6.00pm then you may wish to extend the times, but this does mean that someone has to stay on duty just to check in a very few stragglers at the end.

Choosing a date checklist

❑ Avoid school holidays or half terms, cold weather, other event dates, exam time, sporting fixtures.

❑ Choose a weekend.

❑ Be flexible with the times.

How to delegate or make the event more manageable

If your event is intended to encompass schools from one county or more you will need to share the responsibilities. For an event the size of one (non-metropolitan) city or just one region (e.g. North, South, East, etc.), you may be able to manage the work within your own organising group.

If you decide that you will need help look at the list of participating schools and break it down into areas. A small town with three schools and three or four village schools surrounding it may naturally fall into one area. A city may need to be divided into two, three or four areas of six or eight schools each.

Area Organisers

Within each area there needs to be appointed one area organiser. This person will oversee each participating school in his or her area, establish which schools will have loos, refreshments or other activities available, act as a distribution point for event material and be responsible for the area advertising campaign. They will also be the first point of contact for queries and information.

At an appropriate time it may be helpful to hold a meeting to bring all the area organisers together and clarify their responsibilities and give them instructions and advice straight from the horse's mouth as it were. It would be impossible to meet with every one of the school's organisers, and this helps to dissipate information more efficiently. You will probably need a back up of written instructions.

It may also be that advertising could overlap from one area to another and demarcation lines need to be agreed so as not to waste publicity material and time in duplication. Just an opportunity to share information and pool ideas can be very valuable. Everyone has a slightly different way of looking at things, has different contacts or skills and can give a fresh angle on an established thought. Don't waste your resources.

School Organisers

The area organisers in turn delegate certain responsibilities to the schools themselves.

Each school must set up a rota of officials to sign in all the cyclists. It is more friendly as well as more efficient to ensure that there are at least two people on duty at once. Each pair should work a minimum of one hour and probably a maximum of three in a stretch. The signing in procedure is given in detail further on in the chapter.

If toilet facilities are available, and this need not be at every school, then arrangements should be made to check cleanliness and supplies at regular intervals throughout the day. Signs need to be made and erected before the start of the event.

Refreshments are very welcome, and a necessity if the weather is hot. A drinks stall also provides an additional fundraiser for the school. As well as all the on-the-day duties, the school organiser is also

---

Delegation checklist

❑ Use levels of delegation appropriate to the size of the event.

❑ Appoint area organisers and/or schools organisers.

❑ Area organisers are like regional managers and distributors.

❑ Schools organisers are on-site managers.

❑ Consider holding one information meeting for all.

---

responsible for collecting all the money and returning it to the central collection account as described below.

Selling points

There is much about this event to commend it. To my mind anything that helps children to learn a healthy life style has to be encouraged. It has been suggested that television has a lot to answer for the sedentary existence that many young people now choose to adopt. Recent tests on teenagers have shown that in many cases their cardiovascular systems have not developed to the size that one would expect, due to lack of exercise as children. A regular and enjoyable sporting activity started when young can become the blueprint for life as an adult.

Cycling provides good cardiovascular exercise without putting undue stresses and strains on joints. It involves speed and excitement, which for young people is almost obligatory. It gets people out of the home and into some fresh air. Nearly all children own a bike of some sort from about the age of six or seven so a cycling event rarely involves any extra special equipment. And, speaking as one who does not even own a bicycle, it might just act as the catalyst for adults to come back to cycling and do something as a family group.

From the schools' point of view a formal cycle ride can provide the focus for learning the relevant sections of the *Highway Code* and how to practice road safety. It can encourage children to forsake their convenient lifts by car and ride their bikes the two or three miles that it takes to get most children to school as practice for the 'big day'. Environmentally it makes more sense too which is quite probably an added attraction for school children; we have all noticed how aware they are of their surroundings and their responsibilities towards the environment.

For their part perhaps schools can take the opportunity to ensure that bike sheds are well maintained with modern fittings to keep bicycles undamaged and out of the wet with locking facilities to ensure that their pupils'

Selling points checklist

❑ Provides children with encouragement to lead healthier life styles.

❑ Good outdoor exercise.

❑ No special equipment needed.

❑ Family activity.

❑ Provides focus for road/traffic education.

❑ Environmentally advantageous.

❑ Makes schools re-examine their bike storage provision.

❑ Helps children feel involved and may instil a feeling of responsibility.

prized method of transport does not grow legs and disappear. It is not a good incentive to provide a leaky tin shack with an inadequate selection of stands and every opportunity for the passing thief.

More indirectly, if children have been personally involved in raising money for a specific project, especially if it is for something they requested or had a hand in choosing, they are probably more likely to respect the finished thing and less likely to turn to vandalism.

Finance and legalities

Unless you are, even in part, collecting for one umbrella charitable cause, running a schools cycle ride means that you will be raising funds for multiple purposes (i.e. as many schools as are participating in the event). This does pose a few minor problems involving bank accounts, whom to make cheques payable to and the basic fact that you are likely to be collecting money for a non-registered charitable cause.

These concerns are not insurmountable by any means, but must be addressed carefully to ensure that unforeseen eventualities are catered for.

Running one event of this type, even annually, is not reason enough for rushing out and getting your group registered as a bone-fide charity. You are perfectly at liberty to raise money for charitable causes even if the benefiting organisation is not registered as a charity with the Charity Commission. The tax advantages of being registered will be negligible, as the donations are not being made by Deed of Covenant, are small individually and money will be in a single bank account for such a short time and not earning interest. You are not organising a street collection and you are not organising a public appeal, and anyway in such cases the Public Collections legislation in the Charities Act extends to benevolent organisations as well as to charities. The hassle of getting registered and the duties which you sign up to all tip the balance very clearly in favour of non-registration.

Your group does, however, need to establish itself as a committed group. This can be done by forming an 'informal trust' or – the legally recognised term – a Bare Trust. You don't need lawyers and money to set this up. All you need to do is write a short constitution setting out the intentions of the group... 'collecting money for the purposes of benefiting participating schools, etc...' what you are to be known as, and then list the members of the group and who is to act as signatory for the bank account. That's all.

Your next task is to open the bank account which should be relatively easy if you go armed with the above document. Many banks and building societies have club or society accounts which are not specifically for charitable purposes, and you may find that you fall into this category. Check that the organisation you choose provides free banking for the first year. You may have to re-open an account each year or you may be allowed to send it into 'hibernation' until the next event to prevent you moving into a world of bank charges when year one is up. Terms are infinitely negotiable these days, and it pays to list your requirements and shop around until you are satisfied. The TSB may be a good starting point as they like to be associated with the educational field and sponsor many charitable causes (information true in 1994).

I stated above that you would not be organising a street collection. If you wanted to do so you would need a local authority licence which might be difficult to obtain without a charity registration number. However, there is nothing to stop you having collecting tins available actually on school land.

You must also make arrangements to pay for your administration and publicity costs. This can be achieved in one of three ways.

Firstly, you can arrange to hold back one or two percent of the sponsorship money to cover costs, but this has to be clearly stated on the literature. Secondly you could ask for a small entry fee to be made to be kept separate from the donations. Thirdly you can look for company sponsorship.

There are advantages and disadvantages to all systems. The first makes it necessary that all donations are returned for processing by your organising group. This is time consuming for both the schools organiser and the main group and costs extra in postage. However, this would happen anyway if you were to lift a percentage for another charity, and you might consider that this is the course to take if a dual beneficiary is planned.

The second idea might be advisable if it is purely a schools event. The schools collect the donations and keep them. They then return the sponsorship forms, having kept their own records, so that award winners can be notified and to show how much they raised, together with a cheque for the entry fees which they collect from all cyclists who start the ride from their school.

A problem that you might meet from using either of these two systems is one of left over funds. If you do not spend every last penny, you may be left with cash in your account which means that you cannot close it thereby running the risk of incurring charges. You cannot keep the money yourselves, and clearly you cannot return more money to any one school than they have officially 'earned', and to try to divide a few pounds fairly between 400 to 500 schools is impractical.

The bank or building society might be generous and allow you to keep the extra as a pump-primer for next year as long as you do not make any transactions until the account is officially 'awakened' again or you could opt to spend every last penny on prizes as described below.

The third idea, company sponsorship (described in detail later in this chapter), can solve the banking problem; it is cost efficient, but might add considerable extra work. If searching for company sponsorship starts to look as if it will entail weeks of trailing around and enough rejection slips to paper your bathroom with, then don't bother. This event is not dependent on finding a sponsor to cover all the costs.

Company sponsorship might be available in kind. Newspaper companies might print sponsorship forms and schools lists free of charge. A stationery company might donate the paper. And I have never known an event yet that did not attract at least a couple of donated prizes.

Finance and legal checklist

- ❏ You needn't be a registered charity.
- ❏ You must establish yourselves as an official group using a Bare Trust constitution.
- ❏ You should write a short constitution.
- ❏ Open a bank account but check on free banking facilities first.
- ❏ Choose a system to pay administration costs.
- ❏ Consider company sponsorship in cash or in kind but don't loose sleep over it.

Police

Your event is totally dependent on the availability of public highways, and you have a duty to inform the police of your intentions. Normally you wouldn't have to notify the police until a few weeks before the event, but because this involves school children, bicycles and roads to a large extent it is as well to discuss matters with them well in advance.

Write a letter to the Divisional Commander of the local police force outlining the event in brief and giving the date and times that you plan the event. You should also include a map showing all the schools that are intending to take part. It also helps if you can give an estimate as to how many cyclists they can expect to be using the roads. This is probably pure guess work in the first year, but it might assist if you give a total of the number of pupils attending the participating schools. They can then make an assessment on peak usage times, family groups and so on.

The police may wish to make suggestions to help keep cyclists away from main traffic routes, to use back gates of schools or even that certain schools should not be used at all because of the proximity to dangerous roads. Whatever their involvement, it is important that you listen to the police and adhere to their advice.

You may wish to publish an advice statement from the police on the sponsorship forms indicating that cyclists should wear conspicuous clothing, ride in single file and stay off main roads as far as possible.

Police checklist

❑ Inform the police of your intentions well in advance.

❑ Follow police advice.

❑ Consider including police statement on the sponsorship forms.

❑ The event gives the police a good excuse to check bikes for roadworthiness.

Many schools have a good relationship with the traffic police, welcoming them to instruct pupils on road use, cycling proficiency and how to check bikes for road-worthiness: the cycle ride could be used as a positive tool for the police to insist that they give a talk at each school to those who are taking part.

Safety

Clean water and plastic cups must be available at every school. Dehydration is a very real risk at all sporting events where the participants expend energy for extended periods in warm weather. It is a unpleasant and potentially dangerous experience and totally avoidable if a regular intake of fluid is available.

Remember that groups should be encouraged to ride in single file and to wear cycle helmets. The police indicate that brightly coloured clothes or reflective cross straps or tabards help to ensure that the cyclist, or walker, is visible to other traffic.

Bikes must be reasonably well maintained. Some police forces are prepared to visit schools to teach children how to look after their machines and how to make regular checks. Perhaps a roadworthiness check might be made available at the school during the week leading up to the ride.

Participants should be familiar with the *Highway Code* and, again, maybe this is an opportunity for schools to become involved in a little extracurricular tuition.

Ensure that a first aid box is kept on hand at each school and is available for blisters or sprained ankles and the like. Serious accidents should be recorded and reported to the police if they involve a third party, but it should be made clear on the sponsorship form that the organisers accept no liability in respect of death or injury sustained by any cyclist or walker whilst on public roads during the Sponsored Cycle Ride. Participants are totally responsible for their own actions and bicycles despite your advice.

At the risk of sounding like 'Nanny knows best' and including too much obvious advice in the event literature, schools might like to take on the role of suggesting that children wear sensible clothing in the form of two or three thin layers that can be quickly removed and replaced and carry cagoules if it looks like rain. You might like to give some consideration as to whether children under a certain age have to be accompanied by an adult. This is clearly more important in certain parts of the country than in others.

An event such as this is very safe provided that the people taking part behave responsibly. Other traffic is the main risk, but the route that participants take is entirely up to them, the places that they visit are their choice, and they use their own equipment. At the end of the day all you can do is make suggestions and follow police advice.

Safety checklist

❑ Make sure clean water is available free of charge.

❑ Encourage good cycling practice.

❑ Bikes should not be allowed on the road if not up to standard.

❑ Keep a first aid box and an accident record at all check-in points.

❑ Consider suggesting that schools give clothing advice and decide if children need to be accompanied.

Accessibility

All the little extras described above help to make the event more accessible to families. Children, and many older people, need regular loo stops, variation helps to take away the risk of monotony, and food and drink 'en route' saves the extra effort of picnics. And its not just those of cycling age who can benefit; many keen cyclists take babies of six months and over in baby seats on the back of the bike. A few well advertised baby change facilities might be very welcome and show that you have thought of everyone.

A cycle ride, by definition, might be expected to exclude those of us who are less able and maybe that is true of the very elderly and infirm. However, our local village school has one pupil who has to use a wheel chair and he would be disgusted to think that he could not take part using his own particular mode of transport. Flat Tarmac surfaces are ideal for wheelchairs and my own father who has had to use a chair for over forty years might well have liked to rise to a challenge such as this a few years ago. With a little forethought, those who might like to take part can have their way smoothed a little with your help.

If you know that you will have a wheelchair entrant you need to make suitable arrangements – if you are not sure what is needed ask the person using the chair. She or he will know! Ensuring that check-ins are placed on a level surface with a smooth, step-less approach certainly helps. Where there are doors to negotiate, an entrance of one metre width or more saves skinned knuckles, and at the check-in a desk or table (to get ones knees under) is preferable to a counter type arrangement which means that the wheelchair user has to come up to the table in an uncomfortable sideways movement. Of course, toilet facilities should be made available at ground level wherever possible.

Accessibility checklist

❏ Consider what you will need to make the event accessible to everyone.

❏ Don't rule people out just because of your own assumptions.

❏ Ask what is needed from those who know.

Other charities

Sometimes it might be desirable to combine collecting for individual schools with collecting for another charity. It is probably advisable to restrict the additional beneficiary to just one other organisation or the message can become rather diluted. Perhaps an educational or children's charity, or maybe something topical that has so taken the imaginations of children that they feel a desperate need to help somehow.

Sponsorship money will go to the organising group as before but only half (or an agreed percentage) will be returned to each school, the other half being donated to the chosen organisation.

Marketing and advertising

Marketing the event should not be difficult. Indeed, as stated above, you have a captive audience. You can target each school and be fairly sure that nearly every leaflet will find a home. Head Teachers are often quite prepared to include information in letters going home to parents.

A comprehensive list of participating schools, together with their addresses, needs to be made available unless you are including all schools in a clearly defined area when an Ordinance Survey map should be sufficient. The list, along with sponsorship forms, can be made available directly from the schools and you can ask the children themselves to design posters.

Your main objective will be to make the event seem cohesive and under one organisational group whilst not detracting from the message that each school will benefit individually and strictly in accordance with the number of people who nominate each school.

As I have found in the past, teachers, pupils and parents are very loyal to their own schools and do not like to feel that their school might be losing out to others. The answer, as with so many events, is for each school, not the umbrella group this time, to announce a target figure to be raised from the event, in this way it all seems very pertinent to their own needs. As the pledged donations come in after the cycle ride, everyone can see how near the total is to the target thereby encouraging extra donations, and again showing how their own pupils, parents, teachers, etc. have had a direct impact on their own school.

Other than the direct marketing to the schools themselves, there is very little advertising that is needed. A few posters and sponsorship forms placed in local shops and community centres may bring in a few interested locals, and some well timed press releases help to put the event on the map and might encourage some keen cyclists to join in the event just for the fun of it. Don't forget to publish an address for people to send a SAE for a sponsorship form. You might also send a letter explaining the event to local cycling clubs and ask the major cycle supply shops to display a poster and stock sponsorship forms.

Then there is the question of participant identity. Young children in particular love stickers, and the Church Cycle Ride has a new style sticker produced annually which is proudly displayed on participants' cycles year after year. The sticker is about the diameter of a tea cup with a peel-off backing. If you wanted to follow their example (you could use arm bands, sashes or badges just as well), I suggest that these are given out to each cyclist at the start of the ride rather than making them available with the sponsorship forms. This means that only those who take part are eligible for a sticker, helps prevent waste and keeps costs down. If you run the event as an annual ride you will find, as we do, that people display all their stickers on their bikes showing how many years they have competed. It has the added advantage of showing the police, if they need to know, who is a bone fide participant.

Most events are started by a celebrity actor, politician or celebrity of some sort. You cannot open your event with a VIP cutting the ribbon as the start is not in one particular place. However, you might be able to arrange a five-minute broadcast from a local radio station where a VIP starts the event on air! Each school could have a radio tuned to the appropriate station made available and as the signal is sounded the cyclists starting from that spot could move off. Perhaps the radio station would sponsor your administration costs too. I am sure you would be more likely to attract a big name celebrity to a five-minute job in the studio rather than an hour or two outside in some far flung part of the country. Alternatively, if you wish to keep the event more low key, the Head Teacher from each school could give the signal to move off from each start point. The timing is not crucial and it might help to make each school feel important.

When you have finished the final totting up and you have all your award winners sorted out, you may choose to hold a prize giving ceremony where the celebratory name might be prevailed upon again to present the goodies. You could choose to hold this in the winning school or, if you are operating the event alongside a charity, it might be better to use their local offices. Remember to invite the press and to take your own photographs and write your own report if they fail to turn up on time.

Marketing checklist

❑ Target each pupil through letters going home from school.

❑ Make a comprehensive list of all participating schools available to cyclists so they can work out their routes.

❑ Ask the children themselves to design posters.

❑ Make it clear that each school benefits in direct accordance with how many pupils take part.

❑ Announce target figures and projects.

❑ Include a little local advertising but don't go overboard.

❑ Send press releases to local media.

❑ Consider stickers for all participants.

❑ Decide how you will start the ride.

❑ Decide when and where you will award prizes.

Prizes and awards

As well as the enjoyment of the ride itself and the knowledge that they are helping their nominated school, cyclists should have the opportunity to win something for themselves from the event. People often like to feel that they are competing for something, and if there is the possibility of personal reward at the end then it makes the competition all the more worth while. Advertise the best prizes on the posters, leaflets and in the press releases.

Especially press releases. It is amazing how nothing succeeds like success, as the old saying goes. If one big company is seen to support an event, then others cannot wait to get a slice of the action.

The cycle ride gives all sorts of opportunities for prizes, who should receive them, who should give them and who should pay for them. Spot prizes are advertised in concept only and are offered as a bit of fun and surprise. Clearly, to advertise exactly what they are could mean people contriving to be in a particular place at a particular time.

Prizes can be offered from the proceeds but it is much more cost effective to look for donations. The obvious prize is a bicycle but you might look for cycling equipment, safety helmets, trainers or almost anything that would appeal to school children. If an adult wins a prize then perhaps some department store vouchers might be a good alternative. The schools themselves might wish to present special prizes to their own pupils.

Prizes don't have to be 'things' as such. There could be a special certificate prepared by a calligrapher for the school that raised the most money. The school as a whole has a sense of achievement and others have something to strive for and beat next time.

Suggested categories for prizes

1. The cyclist (and/or walker) who visited the most schools during the time allowed.

2. The school which had the most visits.

3. The cyclist who raised the most money.

4. The school which raised the most money.

5. The youngest/oldest participant.

6. Spot prizes. The hundredth person to visit a particular school or person arriving exactly at mid-day, first person on a lime green bike, etc.

7. School nominated prizewinner. Someone competing despite great difficulties or having built their own bike in metalwork classes!

8. Pupil who encouraged the most entrants. (Needs to be a space on the sponsorship form for the cyclist to enter the name of the pupil that recruited him/her.)

Prizes checklist

❑ Provide a whole gamut of prizes and awards for participants and for the schools.

❑ Look for donated prizes/company sponsorship or provide awards from the entry fees.

❑ Consider beautifully handwritten certificates as well as prizes.

Sponsorship forms

Sponsorship forms should be no bigger than A4. A4 folded into A5 is a convenient size, offering four sides for information and names, or you could try A4 folded into 3 as shown in the illustration on page 146.

On the front you need the name (and logo) of the event, the

SCHOOLS VISITED

To be completed by an official at each school

School	Time	Initials
TOTAL		

School	Time	Initials
TOTAL		

To be completed before start of ride – your details

Name _____

Address _____

Telephone _____

Name and address of the school nominated to benefit

Name _____

Address _____

Name and address of schools organiser to whom this form and money must be returned by (date)

Name _____

Address _____

Official use only	
Schools Organiser	Organising Group

SCHOOLS BIKE RIDE

Date 1996
10.00am – 6.00pm

Bicycle or walk around (Area) schools to raise money for school of your choice and

CHARITY NAME

Name of Sponsor	Address	Sponsorship per School	Donation	Total
Total Money Raised				

Thank You to all who have sponsored the holder of this form

Sponsored Bike Ride information

Bike Ride umbrella organisation

Address and Contact

Police instructions

One idea for the Schools' Bike Ride sponsorship form

date, time and year. Include a sponsorship acknowledgement if necessary. A brief description is helpful such as *'Bicycle or walk around (name of area) schools to raise money for the school of your choice'*. You would add the name of the charity if you are collecting for another organisation too.

Inside you need space for at least 20 sponsors' names and addresses, the sum sponsored per school, a column for donations and another for totals. You should include a brief word about your own organisation and a contact address, how the cycle ride works and a thank you note to the sponsors.

The police will probably ask you to add a paragraph directed at cyclists and walkers to the effect that they should behave in a safe manner, wear the proper clothes and use a well maintained machine.

You also need a space for the cyclist to include their own name, address and telephone number and the name and address of the school that they nominate to benefit from the money that they raise, which will also be the school that the sponsorship money should be returned to. Leave a couple of squares (official use only) to be completed by the schools organiser and the organising group.

The final section should be a series of columns to be completed by the official at each school that the cyclist will visit. Try to include at least thirty rows of three columns, each to include a space for the official stamp, the time of arrival and the initials of the official.

The role of the official at each school on the day

As has been suggested there should be at least two officials on duty at any one time. The check-in point need only be a small table or possibly two if you expect a crowd, well inside the school gates but within view and very clearly signposted. In my experience cyclists tend to arrive in small bunches; rather more and closer together at the start of the event and thinning out, as you might expect, after a few hours. People don't usually mind waiting for their turn as they are glad of the rest.

The officials cannot check in the cyclists except between the published start and finish times. As each cyclist arrives the official should mark their form with the time of arrival, stamp it with a rubber stamp embossed with the name of the school and confirm the details by writing their initials in the appropriate column.

(Most schools have rubber stamps available, if not, they should supply their own as part of the conditions for taking part.)

If a cyclist is starting the event (i.e. this is their first visit to any school), then the official should make a quick check to ensure that the space for the cyclist's own name and address is completed and that she or he has nominated a school. The odds are that the cyclist will start the event from the nominated school and if this is the case then, unless it is already completed, the official should write the name of the appropriate school organiser to whom the money should be returned. (You could supply a list with this information to enable any official at any school to complete this part of the form.)

Having completed the necessary parts of the cyclist's form the officials should then add the cyclist's name and time, together with the nominated school to a cross referenced list kept by the school organiser to be finally returned to the main organising group. This provides a ready reckoner to establish how many visits have been made to the one site. It also helps to provide a record for future use of when the peak visiting times are and the most popular start and finish times. You might wish to adjust the event times or put more officials on duty at certain schools at other events when you see the results.

Some very large schools may need considerably more than two officials to start people off in the first hour or two. The schools themselves should make the decision and might like to keep a record of how many people have asked for sponsorship forms to help them make an informed choice. It might be wise to suggest that schools arrange to have people on 'stand-by' in case things become a bit fraught.

The officials should be responsible for maintaining availability of water and plastic cups. This is particularly important when you have very young and elderly people taking part or if the weather is warm.

On the day checklist

❏ Provide a check-in point easily accessible to all.

❏ Only stamp forms between the official start and finish times.

❏ Officials should complete cyclists' own sponsorship forms and their own record sheets.

❏ Officials should check if a form is complete and correct before allowing a cyclist to start the event from his/her school.

❏ Each school is responsible for providing a rota of enough officials.

❏ Officials are responsible for ensuring a supply of water and cups.

Boosting funds

Obviously the more schools that are visited by one cyclist the more money is raised for the nominated school. On the other hand, the schools that are visited do not benefit from each visit unless they have been specifically nominated by that cyclist.

However, something that has become apparent from the Church Cycle Ride is that people visit specific churches as much to walk around and admire the building as to clock up another visit or because it is on a convenient route. To my surprise I have found that visitors are prepared to spend up to ten minutes resting and looking before they feel that they have to move on. Of course there are those who are really rising to the challenge and seem to be off again as soon as they have the stamp on their forms, but even they cannot expect to ride at full pelt for eight hours.

Now, I am not suggesting that every school is housed in a fascinating medieval building or that the architecture is worth a photograph from every angle, but there are plenty of other interesting opportunities that schools can exploit and they can raise money too!

Bearing in mind that experience shows that people are prepared to wander about but for a maximum of, perhaps, ten minutes, activities or entertainment should be short and sweet, and offered by the children, naturally.

Exhibitions of work might be one obvious suggestion. Buskers, musicians, jugglers, magicians, etc. might be another. Fete activities might offer a third. You could use a lucky dip, a coconut shy or other feats of skill or chance to add a little excitement to the visit. You don't need anything too elaborate with a small charge or just 10p or 15p or even ask for a straight forward donation.

Schools can also boost funds by charging for refreshments (as suggested, water should be available free of charge at all check-in points). Something easy to hold and eat on the move would be most welcome. Wrapped sandwiches and rolls, biscuits, sweets and cans of fizz or squash are ideal and can bring in a not insignificant amount of cash during the course of the day. Anything other than canned drinks, tea or

---

Boosting funds checklist

❑ Encourage schools to add extra entertainment/ attractions.

❑ Cyclists will only spend up to ten minutes at each school so keep activities short.

❑ Provide and charge for refreshments, other than water, but check on Environmental Health regulations.

❑ Use symbols on your list of schools to indicate what is available.

149

wrapped biscuits will be covered by the Food Hygiene regulations. Sandwiches may have to be made on licensed premises (e.g. the school kitchens – look at the chapter on Food in *Organising Local Events'* to check your responsibilities).

There could be a symbol on the list of participating schools against those with extra activities to encourage extra visits. Use the universally recognised symbol of a knife and fork to indicate that food is available and don't forget to state if a school will have toilet facilities open.

After the event

Immediately after the event the final shift of officials should be available to help the school organiser clear up any litter and tidy any equipment away. Someone should be in charge of ensuring that each school is made secure.

The lists of visitors should be collected up and returned to the school organiser. Over the next two or three weeks the sponsorship money should be paid in to the individual schools. It should be emphasised to all students the need to collect their money and pay it in to the appropriate organiser as quickly as possible.

Unless the system is to keep all that is due at each school and forwarding only the admission fees, the money should be paid into a bank account, perhaps the PTA or school rather than an individual's account – although that too would be acceptable providing that proper records are kept by two people. Either when the full amount is collected, or at the end of each week or so, a cheque can then be forwarded to the organising group. You will need to provide a form for each school to make their returns.

Any prize winners need to be contacted and arrangements should be made to present the awards, be it at an official ceremony or the responsibility lying with the winner's school. Don't forget to take photographs where appropriate. Company spon-

---

After the event checklist

❑ Clear any litter and restore the school to its former appearance.

❑ Lock up.

❑ Make the returns and collect the sponsorship money.

❑ According to the system used, money should be paid into the central account or kept by each school.

❑ Decide on an award ceremony.

❑ Contact prize winners.

❑ Send press releases and provide 'photo opportunities'.

❑ Debrief, and write thank you letters.

❑ Consider holding a party and sounding people out for next year.

sors who donated big prizes will expect to see photographs appear together with some editorial in the press.

Finally, when you are satisfied that all loose ends are tidied up, you can send a press release out to the local media and to each participating school so that they can include it in any newsletters stating the final overall figure and how many took part. You should publish the names of the prize winners and offer congratulations. Personal 'thank you' letters to all the organisers are a must and will be much appreciated. You may wish to hold a debriefing, and if you ran a specially big event perhaps a party or a get-together of all the main protagonists would be a welcome idea. And, of course, this gives you the opportunity to sound out everyone's thoughts on whether to go for another, even bigger and even better, ride for next year.

Fifty
Useful Publications

Tax

1 GIFT AID - A Guide for Donors and Charities
available from your local Tax Office.
Inland Revenue booklet No. IR113.

2 Tax Effective Giving
by Michael Norton, published by The Directory of Social Change, available from The Directory of Social Change, Stephenson Way, London, NW1 2DP Tel: 0171-209 5151. Price £7.95

3 A Practical Guide to VAT for Charities
by Kate Sayer, published by The Directory of Social Change, available from The Directory of Social Change, Stephenson Way, London, NW1 2DP Tel: 0171-209 5151. Price £9.95

4 VAT Leaflet 701/1/92
available from H.M. Customs and Excise Office

5 Inland Revenue Leaflets
available free from your local tax office.
IR113 A Guide for Donors and Charities.
IR64 Giving to Charity - How Businesses can get Tax Relief.
IR65 Giving to Charity - How Individuals can get Tax Relief.
IR75 Tax Relief for Charities.

The Charities Act

6 Charities: Law and Practice
by Eizabeth Cairns, published by Sweet and Maxwell, South Quay Plaza, 183 Marsh Wall, London EC14 9FT. Price £46.00

7 Charities: The New Law, The Charities Act 1992
by Fiona Middleton and Stephen Lloyd, published by Jordon and Sons with The Directory of Social Change, available from The Directory of Social Change, Stephenson Way, London, NW1 2DP Tel: 0171-209 5151. Price £19.95

8 Charity Leaflets
available from the Charity Commission.
CC20 Fundraising and Charities
CC21 Starting a Charity
CC25 Charities Acts 1960 and 1985 - Charity Accounts

CC27 Provision of Alcohol on Charity Premises
CC45 Central Register of Charities - Services Available

Other regulations

9   **Guide to Health, Safety and Welfare at Pop Concerts and Similar Events**
     published by HMSO available from your local HMSO Bookshop or by mail from HMSO publications Centre, PO Box 276, London, SW8 5DT. Price £10

10   **Voluntary But Not Amateur: A Guide to the Law for Voluntary Organisations and Community Groups**
     by Duncan Forbes, Ruth Hayes and Jacki Reason published by the London Voluntary Services Council, available from the Directory of Social Change, Stephenson Way, London, NW1 2DP Tel: 0171-209 5151. Price £12.95

11   **'And Judy Will Run the Cake Stall'**
     available free of charge with a SAE from Parkinson Cowen Brochure Services, 636 Bristol Road South, Birmingham, B31 2JR

12   **The Food Safety Act, 1990 and You - A Guide for the Food Industry**
     published by H.M.Government, available from Food Sense, London SE99 7TT Tel: 0181-694 8862

13   **Guidelines for the Catering Industry on the Food Hygiene (Amendment) Regulations 1990 and 1991**
     published by the Department of Health, available from HMSO Bookshops

14   **The Food Hygiene (Markets, Stalls and Delivery Vehicles) Regulations 1996 as Amended by the Food Hygiene (Amendment) Regulations 1990**
     published by Eaton Publications, P.O. Box 34, Walton-on-Thames, Surrey, Tel: 01932-229001

15   **Essentials of Health and Safety at Work**
     published by the Health and Safety Executive, available from HMSO Bookshops

16   **Lotteries and Amusements Act, 1976 - Cat No. BL5**
     published by Shaw and Sons Ltd, Shaway House, Lower Syndham, SE26 5AE

17   **Guide to Health, Safety and Welfare at Pop Concerts and Other Similar Events**
     available from the Health and Safety Executive, Baynards House, 1 Chepstow Place, London W2 4TF

18   **Recreation and the Law**
     by Valerie Collins, published by E & F N Spon, 11 New Fetter Lane, London EC4P 4EE. Price £13.95

19   **HSE Guidance Note PM76 - inflatable castles**
     available from HMSO. Tel: 0121-200 2461

Fundraising for Schools

20 **School Fundraising - what you need to know**
by Anne Mountfield, published by The Directory of Social Change, available from The Directory of Social Change, Stephenson Way, London, NW1 2DP Tel: 0171-209 5151. Price £9.95

Events and Ideas

21 **Organising Local Events**
by Sarah Passingham, published by The Directory of Social Change, available from The Directory of Social Change, Stephenson Way, London, NW1 2DP Tel: 0171-209 5151. Price £7.95

22 **Tried and Tested Ideas for Raising Money Locally**
published by The Directory of Social Change, available from The Directory of Social Change, Stephenson Way, London, NW1 2DP Tel: 0171-209 5151. Price £8.95

23 **Code of Practice for Outdoor Events (other than Pop Concerts and Raves)**
published by the National Outdoor Events Association, 7 Hamilton Way, Wallington, Surrey SM6 9NJ. Tel: 0181-669 8121. Price £40 to non-members

24 **The Complete Fundraising Handbook**
by Sam Clarke, published by the Directory of Social Change, Stephenson Way, London, NW1 2DP Tel: 0171-209 5151. Price £9.95

25 **How to Raise Funds Sponsorship**
by Chriss McCallum, published by How To Books, Plymbridge House, Estover Road, Plymouth PL6 7PZ. Price £7.99

26 **The Road Race Handbook**
published by the British Athletic Federation Ltd, Edgebaston House, 3 Duchess Place, Hagley Road, Edgebaston, Birmingham B16 8NM. Tel: 0121-4564050. Price £3.00

Committees and organising groups

27 **Getting Organised**
by Christine Holloway and Shirely Otto, published by the National Council of Voluntary Organisations, available from the Directory of Social Change, Stephenson Way, London, NW1 2DP Tel: 0171-209 5151. Price £5.95

28 **Starting and Running a Voluntary Group**
by Sally Capper, Judith Unell and Anne Weyman published by the National Council of Voluntary Organisations, available from the Directory of Social Change, Stephenson Way, London, NW1 2DP Tel: 0171-209 5151. Price £3.95

29 **Just About Managing**
by Sandy Merritt Adirondack published by the London Voluntary Service Council, available from the Directory of Social Change, Stephenson Way, London, NW1 2DP Tel: 0171-209 5151. Price £10.95

155

30 **The Management of Voluntary Organisations**
published by Croner Publications Ltd. Croner House, London
Road, Kingston-upon-Thames, Surrey, KT2 6SR. Tel: 0181-547
3333. This is a very large, loose-leaf for easy update, publication
and due to its rather high cost probably best looked for in a
library. It is well worth studying on all sorts of topics.

Professional entertainers and help

31 **Showcall Directory**
compiled and published by the Stage and Television Today, 47
Bermondsey Street, London, SE1 3XT Tel: 0171-403 1818. Price £18.00

32 **The Showman's Directory**
compiled and published by Lance Publications, Brook House, Mint
Street, Godalming, Surrey GU7 1HE Tel. 01483-422184. Price £17.00

33 **The White Book**
published by Birdhurst Ltd, P.O. Box 55, Staines, Middlesex, TW18
4UG. Tel: 01784 464441. Price £45.00

Publicity and Marketing

34 **Marketing: A Handbook for Charities**
by Dorothy and Alistair McIntosh published by the Directory of Social
Change, Stephenson Way, London, NW1 2DP Tel: 0171-209 5151.
Price £7.95

35 **The D.I.Y. Guide to Public Relations**
by Moi Ali, published by the Directory of Social Change,
Stephenson Way, London, NW1 2DP Tel: 0171-209 5151. Price
£12.50

36 **Sell Space to Make Money**
by Audrey Semple, published by the Directory of Social Change,
Stephenson Way, London, NW1 2DP Tel: 0171-209 5151. Price
£2.95

37 **A Media Handbook for Charities**
available 1996, by Karina Holly published by the Directory of Social
Change, Stephenson Way, London, NW1 2DP Tel: 0171-209 5151.
Price £12.50

38 **The Directory of Volunteering and Employment Opportunities
1995/6 edition**
edited by Jan Brownfoot and Frances Wilks, published by the
Directory of Social Change, Stephenson Way, London, NW1 2DP
Tel: 0171-209 5151. Price £9.95.

Volunteers

39 **Essential Volunteer Management**
by Rick Lynch and Steve McAuley, published by the Directory of Social
Change, Stephenson Way, London, NW1 2DP Tel: 0171-209 5151.
Price £12.95.

40 The Voluntary Agencies Directory
compiled and published by the National Council of Voluntary Organisations, available from the Directory of Social Change, Stephenson Way, London, NW1 2DP Tel: 071-209 5151. Price £10.95

41 Volunteer Centre UK Publications
A range of handbooks, good practice guides, resource packs and research papers is available from the Volunteer Centre UK, Carriage Row, 18 Eversholt Street, London NW1 1BU Tel: 0171-383 9888.

Sponsorship

42 Association for Business Sponsorship of the Arts / WH Smith Sponsorship Manual
available through W.H.S. Smith stores. Price £14.95

43 A Guide to Company Giving 1993 Edition
edited by Michael and Nicola Eastwood, published by the Directory of Social Change, Stephenson Way, London, NW1 2DP Tel: 0171-209 5151. Price £15.95

44 The Major Companies Guide
edited by David Casson, published by the Directory of Social Change, Stephenson Way, London, NW1 2DP Tel: 0171-209 5151. Price £14.95

45 Hollis Sponsorship and Donations Yearbook
published by Hollis Directories, Contact House, Lower Hampton Road, Sunbury-on-Thames, Middlesex TW16 5HC Tel: 01932 784781. Price £75.00

46 The Arts Funding Guide
compiled by Anne-Marie Doulton, published by the Directory of Social Change, Stephenson Way, London, NW1 2DP Tel: 0171-209 5151. Price £15.95

47 The London Grants Guide
edited by Lucy Stubbs, published by the Directory of Social Change, Stephenson Way, London, NW1 2DP Tel: 0171-209 5151. Price £12.50

48 West Midlands Grants Guide
edited by Nicola Eastwood and Daren Felgate, published by the Directory of Social Change, Stephenson Way, London, NW1 2DP Tel: 0171-209 5151. Price £9.95

Special Needs - both participatory or as audience

49 The Creative Tree
edited by Gina Levete, published by Michael Russell (Publishing) Ltd, The Chantry, Wilton, Salisbury, Wiltshire. Price £7.95

50 Arts for Everyone
by Anne Pearson, published by the Carnegie Trust, available from Centre on Environment for the Handicapped, 126 Albert Street, London NW1 7NF. Price £6.00

Thirty-Five
Useful Addresses

Street Processions

1   **Peeks of Bournmouth Ltd**
Riverside Lane,
Tuckton, Christchurch,
Bournemouth, Dorset BH6 3LD
Tel: (01202) 4177777
*Complete fundraising packages
including games, novelties,
Balloons, etc.*

2   **Wall's Carnival Stores Ltd**
155/161 Caversham Road,
Reading, Berkshire RG1 8BB
Tel: (01734) 586727
*Fundraising packages, as above -
also balloon gas*

3   **Carousel Fun Fairs Agency**
Plot 24, The Plantation,
West Park Road,
Newchapel, Surrey RH7 6HT
Tel: (01342) 717707
*Dozens of fairground
entertainments to hire and book*

4   **Event Services Ltd**
The Old Foundry,
Brow Mills Road,
Hipperholme, Halifax,
West Yorkshire HX3 8BZ
Tel: 01422 204114
Complete events service

Music Events

5   **The National Outdoor
Events Association**
7 Hamilton Way,
Wallington, Surrey SM6 9NJ
Tel: 0181 669 8121
*The Industry Forum
representing buyers (local
authorities, show organisers etc.)*

*and suppliers of equipment and
services for outdoor events*

6   **Ticketshop**
13, Cremyll Road,
Reading, Berkshire RG1 8NQ
Tel: 01734 599234
Official tickets and publicity

7   **Performing Arts Management
Ltd.**
Canal 7, Clarence Mill,
Bollington, Macclesfield,
Cheshire SK10 5JZ
Tel: 01625 575681
Classical music events organisers

8   **Showground Associates**
Laurels Farm,
Worstead, Norfolk NR28 9RW
Tel: 01692 536025
*Kayam festival tent hire,
equipment and management team*

Orienteering

9   **British Orienteering
Federation**
Riversdale,
Dale Road North,
Darley Dale, Matlock,
Derbyshire DE4 2HX
Tel: 01629 734042
*All you need to know about
orienteering. List of local clubs*

10 **Ultrasport**
The Orienteers' Shop,
4 St Mary's Street,
Newport,
Shropshire TF10 7AB
Tel: 01952 813918
*Suppliers of orienteering
equipment*

11 **Compass Sport – the orienteer**
Compass Sport Publications
37 Sandycoombe Road,
Twickenham TW1 2LR
Tel: 0181-892 9429
National orienteering magazine

General Infrastructure

12 **RAC Signs Service**
RAC House, M1 Cross,
Brent Terrace, London NW2 1LT
Tel: 0800 234810 (Freephone)
*Highway signs and planning
permission*

13 **AA Signs Service**
Fanum House,
Dogkennel Lane,
Halesowen,
West Midlands B63 3BT
Tel: 0121 501
*Highway signs and planning
permission*

14 **GKN Quickform
(Birmingham)**
Tel: 021 7063399 for your nearest
office
Crowd control barriers and fencing

15 **SGB Readyfence**
Tel: 0181 628 3400 for your
nearest office
All types of temporary fencing

16 **The Amazing Bunting
Company**
PO Box 274,
Northampton NN3 4AD
Tel: 01604 786655
*As stated, bunting and other types
of bazaar and fair equipment*

17 **Restroom Rentals / The
Search Group**
Tel: 01532 639081 for your
nearest office
Lavatories

18 **Pilot Hire Ltd.**
Wimpey Estate, Lancaster
Road,
Southall, Middlesex UB1 1NR
Tel: 0181 574 3882
*Lavatories including disabled
facilities*

19 **Geerings of Ashford Ltd.**
Cobbs Wood House,
Chart Road, Ashford,
Kent TN23 1EP
Tel: 01233 633366
*Full publicity service including
catalogues and programmes*

20 **Nipperbout**
84 Clonmell Road,
London N17 6JU
Tel: 0181 801 0148
Mobile creche / childcare

Regulations

21 **Gaming Board of Great Britain**
Berkshire House,
168-173 High holborn,
London WC1V 7AA
Tel: 0171 240 0821
*Advice and registration for all forms
of lotteries where prizes are offered
over £2,000*

22 **Customs and Excise**
New Kings Beam House,
22 Upper Ground,
London SE1 9PJ
Tel: 0171 620 1313
Advice on VAT or your local office

23 **The Performing Rights
Society Ltd.**
29-33 Berners Street,
London W1P 4AA
Tel: 0171 580 5544
*Advice on fees that may be payable
for live music.*

A Few Funding Sources

24 **The Arts Council**
England
14 Great Peter Street,
London SW1P 3NQ
Tel: 0171-333 0100
Scotland
12 Manor Place,
Edinburgh EH3 7DD
Tel: 0131-226 6051
Wales
Holst House, Museum Place,
Cardiff CF1 3NX
Tel: 01222-394711

Northern Ireland
181a Stranmills Road,
Northern Ireland BT9 5DU
Tel: 01232 381591

25 **Crafts Council**
44a Pentonville Road,
Islington
London N1 9BY
Tel: 0171 278 7700

26 **London Chamber of Commerce and Industry**
69 Cannon Street,
London EC4N 5AB
Tel: 0171 248 4444

27 **The Sports Council England**
16 Upper Woburn Place,
London WC1H 0QP.
Tel: 0171 388 1277
Scotland
Caledonia House, South Gyle,
Edinburgh EH12 9DQ
Tel: 0131-317 7200
Wales
Welsh Institute of Sport,
Sophia Gardens,
Cardiff CF1 9FW
Tel: 01222-397571
Northern Ireland
House of Sport,
Upper Malone Road,
Belfast BT9 5LA
Tel: 01232-381222

Charitable Information

28 **Central Register of Charities**
St. Alban's House,
57/60 Haymarket,
London SW1Y 4QX
Tel: 0171 210 3000
Register of all charities

29 **Charity Commission**
St Alban's House,
57/60 Haymarket,
London SW1Y 4QX
Tel: 0171 210 4405
Advice and numerous leaflets on all charitable concerns

30 **National Council for Voluntary Organisations**
Regent's Warf,
All Saint's Street,
London N1 9RL
Tel: 071 713 6161

31 **Charities Aid Foundation**
48 Pembury Road,
Tonbridge,
Kent TN9 2JD
Tel: (017327) 713333
More charity advice

32 **National Federation of Women's Institutes**
104 New King's Road,
London SW6 4LY
Tel: 0171 371 9300
Information on local groups

33 **Community Matters**
8–9 Upper Street,
London N1 0PQ
Tel: 0171-226 0189
The national association of community associations and organisations

34 **National Association of Councils of Voluntary Service**
3rd Floor, Arundel Court
177 Arundel Street,
Sheffield S1 2NV
Tel: 01742-786636
Can provide you with the address of your local Voluntary Service Council which is a good starting point for information on local charities and voluntary organisations

35 **National Association of Volunteer Bureaux**
St Peter's College,
College Road, Saltley,
Birmingham B8 3TE
Tel: 0121-327 0265
Can provide you with the address of your local volunteer bureau which is one starting point for recruiting volunteers